Teen pregnancy and parenting

DATE DUE

Teen Pregnancy and Parenting

Other Books in the Current Controversies Series

Teen Pregnancy and Parenting

Lisa Krueger, Book Editor

GREENHAVEN PRESS
A part of Gale, Cengage Learning

GALE
CENGAGE Learning™

Detroit • New York • San Francisco • New Haven, Conn • Waterville, Maine • London

GALE
CENGAGE Learning

Christine Nasso, *Publisher*
Elizabeth Des Chenes, *Managing Editor*

For more information, contact:
Greenhaven Press
27500 Drake Rd.
Farmington Hills, MI 48331-3535
Or you can visit our Internet site at gale.cengage.com

LIBRARY OF CONGRESS CATALOGING-IN-PUBLICATION DATA

Teen pregnancy and parenting / Lisa Krueger, book editor.
    p. cm. -- (Current controversies)
    Includes bibliographical references and index.
    ISBN 978-0-7377-4923-6 (hbk.) -- ISBN 978-0-7377-4924-3 (pbk.)
    1. Teenage pregnancy--Juvenile literature. 2. Teenage parents--Juvenile literature. 3. Teenagers--Sexual behavior--Juvenile literature. I. Krueger, Lisa.
    HQ759.4.T4252 2010
    306.874'3--dc22

                                                          2010030777

Printed in the United States of America
1 2 3 4 5 6 7 14 13 12 11 10

Contents

Teenagers are routinely exposed to sexual content in the media. Instead of reaching out to their parents for guidance regarding sex, teens tend to push their parents away. The advice and compassion that parents provide can help teens make responsible decisions when it comes to sex, drugs, and alcohol.

Chapter 3: What Challenges Do Teen Parents Encounter?

Chapter 4: Should Parental Consent Be a Requirement?

Foreword

By definition, controversies are "discussions of questions in which opposing opinions clash" (*Webster's Twentieth Century Dictionary Unabridged*). Few would deny that controversies are a pervasive part of the human condition and exist on virtually every level of human enterprise. Controversies transpire between individuals and among groups, within nations and between nations. Controversies supply the grist necessary for progress by providing challenges and challengers to the status quo. They also create atmospheres where strife and warfare can flourish. A world without controversies would be a peaceful world; but it also would be, by and large, static and prosaic.

The Series' Purpose

The purpose of the *Current Controversies* series is to explore many of the social, political, and economic controversies dominating the national and international scenes today. Titles selected for inclusion in the series are highly focused and specific. For example, from the larger category of criminal justice, *Current Controversies* deals with specific topics such as police brutality, gun control, white collar crime, and others. The debates in *Current Controversies* also are presented in a useful, timeless fashion. Articles and book excerpts included in each title are selected if they contribute valuable, long-range ideas to the overall debate. And wherever possible, current information is enhanced with historical documents and other relevant materials. Thus, while individual titles are current in focus, every effort is made to ensure that they will not become quickly outdated. Books in the *Current Controversies* series will remain important resources for librarians, teachers, and students for many years.

In addition to keeping the titles focused and specific, great care is taken in the editorial format of each book in the series. Book introductions and chapter prefaces are offered to provide background material for readers. Chapters are organized around several key questions that are answered with diverse opinions representing all points on the political spectrum. Materials in each chapter include opinions in which authors clearly disagree as well as alternative opinions in which authors may agree on a broader issue but disagree on the possible solutions. In this way, the content of each volume in *Current Controversies* mirrors the mosaic of opinions encountered in society. Readers will quickly realize that there are many viable answers to these complex issues. By questioning each author's conclusions, students and casual readers can begin to develop the critical thinking skills so important to evaluating opinionated material.

Current Controversies is also ideal for controlled research. Each anthology in the series is composed of primary sources taken from a wide gamut of informational categories including periodicals, newspapers, books, U.S. and foreign government documents, and the publications of private and public organizations. Readers will find factual support for reports, debates, and research papers covering all areas of important issues. In addition, an annotated table of contents, an index, a book and periodical bibliography, and a list of organizations to contact are included in each book to expedite further research.

Perhaps more than ever before in history, people are confronted with diverse and contradictory information. During the Persian Gulf War, for example, the public was not only treated to minute-to-minute coverage of the war, it was also inundated with critiques of the coverage and countless analyses of the factors motivating U.S. involvement. Being able to sort through the plethora of opinions accompanying today's major issues, and to draw one's own conclusions, can be a complicated and frustrating struggle. It is the editors' hope that *Current Controversies* will help readers with this struggle.

Introduction

> *"Adequate housing often leads to healthier pregnancies and more positive childhoods for the children."*

A dequate housing can be a challenge for pregnant and parenting teens. Teen parents may live with family members, get their own place, live in a group home, find refuge at a shelter, or become homeless. Pregnant and parenting teens face many challenges, and without adequate housing their abilities to provide for themselves and their children are limited.

Pregnant and parenting teens who have supportive family members may choose to continue living with their families. The support pregnant and parenting teens receive from family members can help them reach their educational goals, gain employment, and satisfy their basic needs. However, living with family members is not always an option for teen parents. The parents of a teen parent may ask them to leave home due to disappointment, finances, or dislike of the teen's partner. These teens may also leave home on their own due to overcrowding, abuse, financial difficulty, or drug and alcohol dependency.

Teen parents who are fortunate enough to secure their own housing learn independent living skills. However, teens living on their own often struggle to secure housing. To do so, teens need to show proof of income, rental history, and undergo a credit check. Furthermore, securing housing that is affordable and safe can be a challenge for teen parents, but it is possible. Once teen parents secure housing, they often juggle paying the bills, parenting, working, and attending school all at once. To lessen the financial strain, some teens live with a roommate. By living with a roommate, teens can share expenses, but they also share living space, which can lead to additional stress. Some teen mothers may also decide to share housing with their baby's father or a significant other.

Pregnant and parenting teens who do not live with family members or do not have a place of their own often turn to group homes. Group homes for pregnant and parenting teens offer housing to individuals who would otherwise have no place to live. The types of services offered by group homes for pregnant and parenting teens vary. Some may offer counseling, supervision, assistance with job placement, transportation, and information about public assistance. In addition, group homes can play a role in helping teens become self-sufficient, delay subsequent teen pregnancy, and become better parents through counseling and parenting classes. Some group homes may offer housing during pregnancy, while others may offer housing only for parenting teens and their children.

Pregnant and parenting teens unable to live with family members, on their own, with friends, or in group homes become homeless. According to the Society for Social Work and Research, "Homeless teens are at increased risk for low-birth weight babies and high infant-mortality because of inadequate health care, poor dietary habits, and a lack of prenatal care due to their poor economic and social resources. Their problems are exacerbated by a high risk for psychological problems, often as a result of abusive and/or neglectful relationships, victimization, and housing instability." Homeless pregnant and parenting youth often turn to shelters. Shelters do not provide long-term living arrangements; they typically provide a place for the teen and the child to sleep, as well as meals, showers, and access to toiletries. Paid employees and volunteers staff shelters and are funded by religious organizations, community programs, and the federal government. But access to services from a shelter is not always an option for pregnant and parenting teens. Shelters in their area may be at full capacity and unable to accept additional people. Traditional shelters for the homeless and battered women may also turn away teen parents due to their age. If teens do use services offered by a shelter, they must follow the rules and regulations. If teens have issues with alcohol or drug dependency, they may choose not to live in a shelter because their addiction makes it difficult to abide by the rules and regulations. The dangerous result is that pregnant and parenting teens with substance dependencies are at a greater risk for being homeless. Safety is a serious issue for pregnant and parenting teens who are homeless. Living on the streets can subject teens and their children to crime, sexual abuse, and unsanitary living conditions.

Teen parents are more likely to have difficulty securing housing than older parents do. Adequate housing often leads to healthier pregnancies and more positive childhoods for the children. Teen parents who have adequate housing are able to take responsibility for themselves and for their child or children. The viewpoints in *Current Controversies: Teen Pregnancy and Parenting* examine these issues in today's society in the following chapters: Does Sex Education Reduce Teen Pregnancy? Does Pop Culture Contribute to Teen Pregnancy? What Challenges Do Teen Parents Encounter? and Should Parental Consent Be a Requirement for Decisions Involving Teen Pregnancy? The wide range of opinions found in these chapters underscores many of the obstacles pregnant and parenting teens face today.

CHAPTER 1

Does Sex Education Reduce Teen Pregnancy?

Chapter Preface

The 2008 presidential election became heated when the campaign of Republican presidential nominee, John McCain, ran an ad criticizing Democratic presidential nominee Barack Obama for his vote for comprehensive sex education in grades K-12. The ad introduced the idea of "'comprehensive sex education' to kindergartners." The announcer then says, "Learning about sex before learning to read? Barack Obama. Wrong on education. Wrong for your family." Obama's campaign spokesman Bill Burton rebutted the ad stating, "It is shameful and downright perverse for the McCain campaign to use a bill that was written to protect young children from sexual predators as a recycled and discredited political attack against a father of two young girls." The legislation in question supported teaching kindergartners about inappropriate touching to help them protect themselves from pedophiles. Obama is a supporter of age appropriate and science-based sex education. The divide between conservatives and liberals on sex education was demonstrated through the controversy surrounding the campaign ad.

The appropriate age to educate school children about sex and the content of sex education in schools has been debated for decades by parents, educators, and government authorities. The administration of former president George W. Bush allocated millions of federal dollars to fund abstinence education. This curriculum teaches youth to abstain from sex. Soon after taking office, President Obama's administration cut funding allocated to abstinence education to make way for comprehensive sex education. This curriculum in public schools can cover a range of topics, including abstinence, birth control, access to contraceptives, resisting peer pressure, sexually transmitted diseases (STDs), sexual abuse, sexual orientation, and abortion.

The content of sex education varies because each state, community, and school district throughout the United States tailors the sex education programs taught in their public schools. According to Molly Masland in a 2010 MSNBC article titled "Carnal Knowledge: The Sex Ed Debate," "Currently 18 states and the District of Columbia require schools to provide sex education and 32 do not. In some states, such as Louisiana, kids might learn about HIV/AIDS, but not about any other STDs or how to prevent pregnancy. In other states, like Washington, teens receive information on everything from birth control pills to homosexuality." Public school districts must abide by current state and federal legislation prior to implementing sex education programs. Both abstinence and comprehensive sex education policies strive to prepare youth for decisions involving their sexuality. Lawmakers on both sides of the aisle want to reduce certain outcomes of sexual behavior, such as teen pregnancy and sexually transmitted diseases. They also want today's youth to have healthy and positive sexual relationships throughout their lives. Finding common ground on the content of sex education programs in public schools remains a challenge for lawmakers. Agreeing on legislation for sex education in public schools is not an easy task because cultural, moral, and religious views are thrown into the mix. The viewpoints in the following chapter explore the effectiveness of sex education in today's society.

Parents Can Help Their Teen Make Informed Decisions by Having the Sex Talk

Niesha Lofing

Niesha Lofing is a staff writer at the Sacramento Bee.

D o you think your teen is having sex? Many parents would say no.

The harsh reality is that only about half of those parents would be right.

Children are engaging in sex at younger ages than in the past, experts say, and research indicates that about 40 percent to 50 percent of 15- and 16-year-olds in California are having sex.

Combine that with a steady increase in sexually transmitted diseases [STDs] among teenagers and a rising teen birth rate, and you have a growing need for parents to educate their children.

"Comprehensive sex education really makes a difference," said Dr. Glennah Trochet, Sacramento County's public health officer. "People always think teens aren't influenced by their parents, but studies show that what their parents tell them, especially if they are very clear, really does influence young people."

Sacramento County has essentially had an epidemic of chlamydia and gonorrhea among 15-to-24-year-olds for the past nine years [2001–09], she said.

About one of every 25 females and one of every 80 males ages 15 to 19 in Sacramento County had a reported case of chlamydia or gonorrhea in 2008, according to the state Department of Public Health. And those are only the reported cases, said Trochet, who explained that people may go for years without knowing they have a disease.

Sacramento County ranked fourth and third in rates of chlamydia and gonorrhea, respectively, among California counties last year [2008].

"Young people are having unprotected sex, and we need to do a better job of sex education and maybe getting kids to delay sexual activity," Trochet said.

Birth rates among 15-to-19-year-olds also rose to 38.8 per 1,000 in Sacramento County last year, up from 37 per 1,000 in 2006, mirroring a national trend.

Given those statistics, what's a parent to do?

Start early: Age 10 or 11 is not too young to start the discussions.

Start Talking Now

"Parents should know that even if their children are not sexually active, they probably are exposed to peer groups who are sexually active," said Dr. Angela Rosas, a pediatric gynecologist with the Children's Specialists Medical Group of Sacramento. "Questions will come up."

Here is some advice from the pros on having these critical conversations.

Start early: Age 10 or 11 is not too young to start the discussions, said Dr. Julius Licata, a clinical psychologist in Orefield, Pa., who runs *www.teencentral.net*, a Web site that offers teens anonymous access to expert counseling and advice.

"I'm seeing kids 13 and 14 saying they have had multiple sex acts with people," he said.

If questions haven't arisen by pre-adolescence, the parent needs to initiate the conversation.

You may be uncomfortable talking about sex. That's OK. Acknowledge your discomfort while telling your child that this is too important a topic to let embarrassment get in the way.

If a parent doesn't let the child know they're open, (the child will) never come to them.

There's no such thing as the perfect time: Sitting down with your child and saying you're going to talk about the birds and the bees isn't always the best method. Look for "spontaneous" teachable moments—in the car, on a walk. Perhaps you'll notice a pregnant teen at your child's school or happen upon a love scene in a movie while watching with your kids.

Let your child know that you are receptive to questions by saying something like, "I'm always here to listen."

"If a parent doesn't let the child know they're open, (the child will) never come to them," Licata said.

Consider getting a book to help with starting the conversation. Grab your spouse, make it a date night and head to a bookstore or library.

Dozens of books are geared to explaining sex and sexual health for teenagers. Take time to scan the contents and make sure the book reflects your values. Read the book before giving it to your child so you're not caught off-guard by questions he or she may have.

What to say: Be clear about your expectations and your family's stance on abstinence and sex—and the reasoning behind it, experts say.

Start by saying, "I don't think you're ready," then be prepared to state your reasons. Expect to be challenged. Avoid being defensive, hostile or angry.

If a child admits to having had sex, don't freak out. A good response from a parent might be, "I'm a little disappointed that you did, but let's talk about this."

STDs and pregnancy: Go over the potential for contracting a sexually transmitted disease and its long-term effects.

All the unfounded middle-school rumors about STDs that existed when you were a kid still surface in schools. Before the conversation, check out *www.cdc.gov* to get the facts about STDs.

Chlamydia and gonorrhea can cause sterility in women. Syphilis, which also is on the rise among teenagers, can result in permanent neurological problems and even death if left untreated.

Talk with both boys and girls about birth control because both share responsibility, Trochet said.

Abstinence and safe sex: Conversations about abstinence and safe sex don't have to be mutually exclusive, Trochet said.

"Parents sometimes feel uncomfortable talking about safe sex practices because it feels like a double standard," she said. "Research shows that children understand it isn't a double message if you're very clear (about the family's values regarding sex)."

Licata recommends starting this portion of the conversation with this sentence: "You should wait, but if you are going to have sex, you need to practice birth control."

Sexual Abuse

Dating violence isn't readily covered in schools, said Rosas, who also specializes in child abuse and neglect. Parents should begin talking to their children about sexual violence once the child begins socializing outside the home.

"When we talk about sexual violence, it doesn't always mean forceful sexual intercourse," she said. "It can mean an intimidating relationship between two teenagers."

Tell your children that you don't want them to succumb to pressure, that sex should be a choice they make when they feel ready. Be aware that boys can be vulnerable to pressure from friends and from aggressive girls.

Be on the lookout if one teenager is being domineering and hypervigilant, one of the first signs of an abusive relationship, Rosas said. Abusers also often try to control the other person by limiting contact with others.

Behavioral changes such as sadness, depression and crying without reason are indicators of an abusive relationship.

Hypotheticals are a good way to start talking about sexual violence. Try, "What would you say if a boy tells you: 'If you loved me, you would do it'?" or, "What if someone is pressuring you into a sex act?"

"Sometimes those conversations are a little easier," she said.

Risk-taking behavior. Teenagers need to know that engaging in alcohol and drug use is strongly linked to sex and sexual assault, Rosas said.

"When they choose to start drinking, they are putting themselves at risk of being sexually assaulted," she said.

By the way, Rosas points out, it is illegal to have sex with someone who cannot consent because he or she is intoxicated.

Reaching Out

Need more help? If you're having trouble getting through to your child, offer a trusted family member, a godparent or a family friend as a resource.

Clergy members can help explain value systems surrounding sex. Pediatricians and family doctors also can provide answers.

Online resources such as *www.teencentral.net* provide a safe, anonymous way for teens to ask questions and get answers within 24 hours from trained counselors. The responses are checked by professionals who have master's degrees or doctorates.

Try *www.advocatesforyouth.org* for more advice on how to talk to your teen about sex and sexual health.

Above all, be receptive. A parent's reaction to a teen or younger child asking about sex can set the tone for how honest the teen will be in the future, said Jodi Campbell, a psychologist who writes curriculum and trains staff for the Teen Central Web site.

"How you react is going to be a litmus test for the future," she said.

Corina Meloche, an Elk Grove single mother, began talking to her daughter, now 12, when she was about 9.

"I definitely plan on following up," she said.

Meloche knows the importance of having an open dialogue about sex with her daughter. The limit of the sex talk provided by Meloche's mother, who has very traditional values, was "wait until you are married," Meloche said.

Meloche's first intimate relationship led to a pregnancy when she was 17. She delivered her daughter on her 18th birthday.

"A gift for adulthood," she said.

She and her boyfriend split up when her daughter was just 8 months old. Meloche hopes that talking about the choices she made will help lead her daughter down a different path.

"I tell my daughter that it could have been done differently," she said. "I tell her, 'You can do it differently and do it better.'"

Abstinence Education Reduces Teen Pregnancy

Christine Kim and Robert E. Rector

Christine Kim earned a master's degree in public policy from Georgetown University in Washington, D.C., and she works as a policy analyst at The Heritage Foundation. Robert E. Rector earned a master's degree in political science from Johns Hopkins University in Baltimore, and he works as a senior research fellow at The Heritage Foundation.

Today's young people face strong peer pressure to engage in risky behavior and must navigate a media and popular culture that endorse—and even glamorize—permissiveness and casual sex. The government implicitly supports these messages by spending more than $1,000,000,000 each year promoting contraception and safe-sex education—12 times what it spends on abstinence education.

Abstinence Education

Although 80% of parents want schools to teach youths to abstain from sexual activity until they are in a committed adult romantic relationship nearing marriage—the core message of abstinence education—these parental values rarely are communicated in the classroom, where the prevailing mentality often condones teen sexual activity as long as the participants use contraceptives. Abstinence usually is mentioned only in passing—if at all. Many who need to learn about the benefits of abstaining from sexual activity during the teenage years never hear them, and those students who choose to abstain fail to receive adequate support for their decisions.

Christine Kim and Robert E. Rector, "The Joy of Abstaining," *USA Today Magazine*, March 2009, pp. 73–75. Copyright © 2009 Society for the Advancement of Education. Reproduced by permission.

Teenage sexual activity is costly, not just for teens, but society. Teens who engage in sexual activity risk a host of negative outcomes, including STD [sexually transmitted disease] infection, emotional and psychological harm, lower educational attainment, and out-of-wedlock childbearing. Genuine abstinence education is crucial to the physical and psycho-emotional well-being of the nation's youth. In addition to teaching the benefits of abstaining from sexual activity until marriage, these initiatives focus on developing character traits that prepare youngsters for future-oriented goals.

Each year, some 2,600,000 teenagers become sexually active—a rate of 7,000 per a day.

When considering Federal funding for abstinence education programs, including maintaining the current definition of "abstaining education," lawmakers should consider all of the available empirical evidence. Teen sexual activity remains a widespread problem confronting the nation. Each year, some 2,600,000 teenagers become sexually active—a rate of 7,000 per day. Among high school students, nearly half report having engaged in sexual activity, and one-third currently are active.

Abstinence Only Programs Work

Abstinence education "teaches abstinence from sexual activity outside marriages as the expected standard for all school age children" and stresses the social, psychological, and health benefits of abstinence. These programs also provide youths with valuable life and decisionmaking skills that lay the foundation for personal responsibility and developing healthy relationships and marriages later in life. Studies have shown that abstinent teens report, on average, better psychological well-being and higher academic achievement than those who are sexually active.

Authentic abstinence programs therefore are crucial to efforts aimed at reducing unwed childbearing and improving youth well-being. Positive behavioral changes were reported in a number of abstinence programs, including:

Reasons of the Heart. Taught over 20 class periods by certified and program-trained health educators, the ROH [Reasons of the Heart] curriculum focuses on individual character development and teaches adolescents the benefits that are associated with abstinence until marriage. A 2008 study evaluated the ROH curriculum's impact on adolescent sexual activity among seventh-grade students in three suburban northern Virginia public schools. The researchers also collected data on a comparison group of seventh-graders in two nearby middle schools that did not participate in the program. Students in those schools instead received the state's standard family life education, which included two videos on HIV-STD prevention and one on abstinence.

Authentic abstinence programs are crucial to efforts aimed at reducing unwed childbearing and improving youth well-being.

The evaluators surveyed seventh-grade students in all five schools before and after the program. They found that, a year after the program, 9.2% of the ROH students who were virgins at the initial survey had initiated sexual activity, compared with 16.4% of the comparison group.

Sex Can Wait. This is a three-series abstinence education program with one series for upper-elementary students, a second for middle-school pupils, and a third for high-school attendees. The program lasts five weeks and offers lessons on character building, life skills, and reproductive biology.

In a 2006 study, researchers compared students who participated to those who received their school districts' standard sex education curricula on two behavioral outcomes: overall abstinence and abstinence during the last 30 days. It was found that, 18 months after the program, upper-elementary students who participated were less likely than nonparticipants to report engaging in recent sexual activity. Among middle-school pupils, participants also were less likely than nonparticipants to report engaging in sexual activity ever and in the preceding month before the 18-month follow-up. Finally, among high school students, the authors found reduced levels of sexual activity in the short term but not in the 18-month follow up.

Heritage Keepers. This is a primary prevention abstinence program for middle- and high-school students offering an interactive three-year, two-level curriculum. To assess its impact, a group of evaluators compared some 1,200 virgin students who attended schools that faithfully implemented the program to some 250 pupils in demographically and geographically comparable schools who did not receive the abstinence intervention. One year after the program, 14.5% of Heritage Keepers students had become sexually active compared with 26.5% of the comparison group. The study found similar results in subsets of African-American pupils, Caucasian students, boys, and girls.

[The For Keeps program] emphasized the psychoemotional and economic consequences of early sexual activity.

Preventing Sexual Activity and Other Risky Behavior

For Keeps. A study published in 2005 evaluated this curriculum as implemented in five urban and two suburban middle schools in the Midwest. Schools were assigned by districts to receive the program, which was part of a countywide teen pregnancy prevention initiative.

Taught by outside facilitators, For Keeps was a five-day curriculum with 40-minute sessions that focused on character development and the benefits of abstinence and tried to help students understand how pregnancy and sexually transmitted diseases can impede their long-term goals. It also emphasized the psychoemotional and economic consequences of early sexual activity. The curriculum was intended both for students who had become sexually active and those who had not.

The evaluation collected data on all pupils through a pre-test survey, and some 2,000 youths (about 70%) responded to a follow-up survey conducted about five months after the program ended. Among youths who engaged in any sexual behavior during the follow-up period, some who participated in For Keeps reported a reduction in "the amount of casual sex, as evidenced by fewer episodes of sex and fewer sexual partners" during the evaluation period, although program participants did not differ from nonparticipants in the likelihood of engaging in sexual activity during the follow-up interval.

Best Friends. The BF [Best Friends] program began in 1987 and operates in about 90 schools across the U.S. The Curriculum is abstinence-based and character-building, designed for girls starting in the sixth grade and offering a variety of services, such as group discussions, mentoring, and community activities. Discussion topics include friendship, love and dating, self-respect, decisionmaking, alcohol and drug abuse, physical fitness and nutrition, and AIDS and STDs. The predominant theme is encouraging youths to abstain from high-risk behaviors and sexual activity.

A 2005 study evaluated the District of Columbia's Best Friends program, which operated in six of the District's 20 middle schools. The study compared data on BF participants to data from the Youth Risk Behavior Surveys (YRBS) conducted for the District. The study found that Best Friends girls were nearly 6.5 times more likely to abstain from sexual activity than YRBS respondents. They also were 2.4 times more likely to abstain from smoking, 8.1 times more likely to abstain from illegal drug use, and 1.9 times more likely to abstain from drinking.

Not Me, Not Now. This is a community-wide abstinence intervention program targeted at children ages nine through 14 in Monroe County, N.Y., which includes the city of Rochester. The program devised a mass communications strategy to promote the abstinence message through paid television and radio advertising, billboards, posters distributed in schools, educational materials for parents, an interactive website, and educational sessions in school and community settings. The program had five objectives: raising awareness of the problem of teen pregnancy; increasing understanding of the negative consequences of teen pregnancy; developing resistance to peer pressure; encouraging parent-child communication; and promoting abstinence among teens. It was effective in reaching early teens, with some 95% of the target audience reporting that they had seen a Not Me, Not Now ad. During the intervention period, there was a statistically significant positive shift in attitudes among preteens and early teens in the county.

Abstinence by Choice. This initiative operated in 20 schools in the Little Rock area of Arkansas. The program targeted seventh-, eighth-, and ninth-grade students and reached about 4,000 youths each year. The curriculum included a five-day workshop with speakers, presentations, skits, videos, and an adult-mentoring component.

A 2001 evaluation found that 5.9% of eighth-grade girls who had participated in Abstinence by Choice a year earlier had initiated sexual activity compared with 10.2% of nonparticipants. Among eighth-grade male participants, 15.8% had initiated sexual activity, compared with 22.8% among nonparticipating boys. (The sexual activity rate of students in the program was compared with the rate of sexual activity among control students in the same grade and schools prior to commencement of the program.)

A Pattern of Reduced Sexual Activity

HIV Risk-Reduction Intervention. A 1998 study evaluated this two-day abstinence-based initiative. The program was delivered to some 200 African-American middle school students in Philadelphia, Pa. Pupils volunteered to participate in a weekend health promotion program, and the volunteers were assigned randomly to an abstinence education program, a safersex education program, or a regular health program (the control group) delivered by trained adult and peer (high school student) facilitators.

The researchers found that, during the three-month follow-up, individuals in the abstinence programs were less likely to report having engaged in recent sexual activity compared with those in the control group, and that they were marginally less likely to report having engaged in recent sexual activity compared to students in the safer-sex program. Although the three groups generally did not differ in their reports of sexual activity in the preceding three months during the six- and 12-month follow-ups, the researchers did report that, among students who had sexual experience before the intervention, those in the safer-sex group reported fewer days of sexual activity on average than students in the control group and the abstinence group.

Stay Smart. Delivered to Boys and Girls Clubs of America participants. SS [Stay Smart] integrated abstinence education with substance-use prevention and incorporated instructions on general life skills. The 12-session curriculum, led by Boys and Girls Club staff, used a postponement approach to early sexual activity and targeted sexually experienced and inexperienced adolescents. Participation was voluntary.

A 1995 study evaluated more than 200 youths who participated in Stay Smart and compared their outcomes to youths who did not participate but still were involved in the Boys and Girls Clubs. The study found that, two years after the program, those who had engaged in prior sexual activity and participated in SS exhibited reduced levels of recent sexual activity compared with nonparticipants.

Project Taking Charge. This was a six-week abstinence curriculum delivered in home economics classes during the school year. It was designed for use in low-income communities with high rates of teen pregnancy. The curriculum contained elements on self-development; basic information about sexual biology (*e.g.*, anatomy, physiology, and pregnancy); vocational goal-setting; family communication; and values instruction on the importance of delaying sexual activity until marriage.

The program was evaluated in Wilmington, Del., and West Point, Miss. Control and experimental groups were created by randomly assigning classrooms either to receive or not to receive the program. The students were assessed immediately before and after the program and at a six-month follow-up. About 23% of participants who were virgins at the pretest initiated sexual activity during the follow-up interval, compared with 50% of the youths in the control group.

Researchers found it notable that youths who had more permissive attitudes were "not only receptive and responsive to the abstinence message in the short run, but that some influence on behavior was also occurring."

Teen Aid and Sex Respect. An evaluation of the Teen Aid and Sex Respect abstinence programs in three Utah school districts reported that certain groups of youths who received these programs delayed the initiation of sexual activity. To determine the effects of the initiatives, students in schools with the abstinence programs were compared with those in similar control schools within the same school districts.

In the aggregate sample, the researchers did not find differences in the rates of sexual initiation between youths who had received abstinence education and those who had not. However, analyzing a cohort of high school students who had fairly permissive attitudes, they found that program participants were one-third less likely to engage in sexual activity one year after the programs compared with nonparticipants. The researchers found it notable that youths who had more permissive attitudes were "not only receptive and responsive to the abstinence message in the short run, but that some influence on behavior was also occurring."

Virginity Pledge Studies

Using the National Longitudinal Study of Adolescent Health, a nationally representative sample of American youth, a number of studies have found that adolescent virginity pledging is associated with delayed or reduced levels of teen sexual activity, other risky behaviors, teen pregnancy, and STDs.

A 1997 study examined a large national sample of teenagers in the seventh through 12th grades. It compared students who had taken a formal virginity pledge with those who had not taken a pledge but otherwise were identical in race, income, school performance, degree of religiousness, and other social and demographic factors. Based on this analysis, the authors found that the level of sexual activity among students who had taken a formal pledge of virginity was one-fourth the level of their counterparts who had not taken a pledge. The researchers also noted that "adolescents who reported having taken a pledge to remain a virgin were at significantly lower risk of making their sexual debut at an early age."

A 2001 study of the virginity pledge movement found a similar association between pledging and delayed sexual activity. According to the authors: "Adolescents who pledge, controlling for all of the usual characteristics of adolescents and their social contexts that are associated with the transition to sex, are much less likely than adolescents who do not pledge, to have intercourse. The delay effect is substantial and robust. Pledging delays intercourse for a long time."

Based on a sample of more than 5,000 students, the latter study reported that taking a virginity pledge was associated with a reduction of approximately one-third in the likelihood of early sexual activity, adjusted for a host of other factors linked to sexual activity rates, including gender, age, physical maturity, parental disapproval of sexual activity, school achievement, and race. When taking a virginity pledge was combined with strong parental disapproval of sexual activity, the probability of initiating sexual activity was reduced by 75% or more.

A 2004 study found virginity pledging was linked to a number of positive life outcomes.

By the third wave of the Adolescent Health survey, administered in 2001, respondents had reached young adulthood, ranging between 19 and 25 years of age. In some cases, the virginity pledge may have been taken up to seven years earlier. Nonetheless, for many respondents, the delaying effect associated with pledging during adolescence appeared to last into young adulthood.

A 2004 study found virginity pledging was linked to a number of positive life outcomes. For example, a 22-year-old white female pledger from an intact family with median levels of family income, academic performance, self-esteem, and religious observance was two-thirds less likely to become pregnant before age 18 and 40% less likely to have a birth out of wedlock compared with a nonpledger with identical characteristics. Strong pledgers with the same characteristics were 40% less likely to initiate sexual activity before age 18 and had an average of one-third fewer sexual partners compared with nonpledgers with the same demographic profile.

Analyzing the same sample of respondents, another study found that the STD rate among pledgers averaged 25% lower than nonpledgers of the same age, gender, race, family background, and religiosity. Significantly, the study showed that virginity pledging was a stronger predictor of STD reduction than condom use on five different measures of STDs. The protective effect of pledging may have extended to other behaviors as well. According to a 2005 study, young adults who took a virginity pledge during adolescence were less likely to engage in a number of risky sexual behaviors compared with those who did not take a pledge.

Now, if we only could get government to pledge its support to abstinence programs instead of free-condoms-for-students initiatives, the teen pregnancy rate might have a chance to take a real plunge.

Comprehensive Sex Education Reduces Teen Pregnancy

Advocates for Youth

The Advocates for Youth organization focuses on helping young people make informed and responsible decisions about their reproductive and sexual health.

Since 1997 the federal government has invested more than $1.5 billion dollars in abstinence-only programs—proven ineffective programs which censor or exclude important information that could help young people protect their health. In fact, until recently, programs which met a strict abstinence-only definition were the only type of sex education eligible for federal funding; no funding existed for comprehensive sex education, which stresses abstinence but also provides information about contraception and condoms.

But the [President Barack] Obama administration's proposed budget for FY10 [Fiscal Year 2010] removed the streams of funding for abstinence-only programs, and created funding for programs which have been *proven effective* at reducing teen pregnancy, delaying sexual activity, or increasing contraceptive use. Not surprisingly, it is comprehensive sex education programs which help youth remain healthy and avoid negative sexual health outcomes. This document explores the research around comprehensive sex education and abstinence-only programs.

Comprehensive Sex Education Has Been Proven Effective

Evaluations of comprehensive sex education programs show that these programs can help youth delay onset of sexual activity, reduce the frequency of sexual activity, reduce [the]

Advocates for Youth, adapted from "Comprehensive Sex Education: Research and Results," September 2009. www.advocatesforyouth.org. Reproduced by permission.

number of sexual partners, and increase condom and contraceptive use. Importantly, the evidence shows youth who receive comprehensive sex education are *not* more likely to become sexually active, increase sexual activity, or experience negative sexual health outcomes. Effective programs exist for youth from a variety of racial, cultural, and socioeconomic backgrounds.

Teens who received comprehensive sex education were 50 percent less likely to experience pregnancy than those who received abstinence-only education.

Researchers studied the National Survey of Family Growth to determine the impact of sexuality education on youth sexual risk-taking for young people ages 15–19, and found that teens who received comprehensive sex education were 50 percent less likely to experience pregnancy than those who received abstinence-only education.

Researcher Douglas Kirby for the National Campaign to End Teen and Unplanned Pregnancy examined studies of prevention programs which had a strong experimental design and used appropriate analysis. Two-thirds of the 48 comprehensive sex ed programs studied had positive effects.

- 40 percent delayed sexual initiation, reduced the number of sexual partners, or increased condom or contraceptive use.

- 30 percent reduced the frequency of sex, including a return to abstinence.

- 60 percent reduced unprotected sex.

Advocates for Youth undertook exhaustive reviews of existing programs to compile a list of programs that have been proven effective by rigorous evaluation. Twenty-six effective programs were identified, twenty-three of which included comprehensive sex education as at least one component of the program. The other programs were early childhood interventions. Of the 23 effective, comprehensive sex education programs:

- Fourteen programs demonstrated a statistically significant delay in the timing of first sex.

- 13 programs showed statistically significant declines in teen pregnancy, HIV, or other STIs [sexually transmitted infections].

- 14 programs helped sexually active youth to increase their use of condoms.

- 9 programs demonstrated success at increasing use of contraception other than condoms.

- 13 programs showed reductions in the number of sex partners and/or increased monogamy among program participants.

- 10 programs helped sexually active youth to reduce the incidence of unprotected sex.

Abstinence-Only Programs Are Inaccurate, Ineffective, and May Even Cause Harm

Where there is ample research to prove that comprehensive sex education programs give young people the tools they need to protect themselves from negative sexual health outcomes, there is *little if any* evidence to show that flawed abstinence-only programs are effective—even at achieving abstinence among teens.

- A congressionally mandated study of four popular abstinence-only programs by the Mathematica found that they were entirely ineffective. Students who participated in the programs were no more likely to abstain from sex than other students.

- Evaluations of publicly funded abstinence-only programs in at least 13 states have shown no positive changes in sexual behaviors over time.

- In December 2004, the U.S. House of Representatives' Committee on Government Reform led by Rep. Henry A. Waxman released a report showing that 80 percent of the most popular federally funded abstinence-only education programs use curricula that distort information about the effectiveness of contraceptives, misrepresent the risks of abortion, blur religion and science, treat stereotypes about girls and boys as scientific fact, and contain basic scientific errors.

- Among youth participating in "virginity pledge" programs, researchers found that among sexually experienced youth, 88 percent broke the pledge and had sex before marriage. Further, among all participants, once pledgers began to have sex, they had more partners in a shorter period of time and were less likely to use contraception or condoms than were their non-pledging peers.

- No abstinence-only program has yet been proven through rigorous evaluation to help youth delay sex for a significant period of time, help youth decrease their number of sex partners, or reduce STI or pregnancy rates among teens.

More than 80 percent of Americans support teaching comprehensive sex education in high schools and in middle or junior high schools.

Public opinion polls consistently show that more than 80 percent of Americans support teaching comprehensive sex education in high schools and in middle or junior high schools. In one poll, 85 percent believed that teens should be taught about birth control and preventing pregnancy; in another, seven in 10 opposed government funding for abstinence-only programs. Support for comprehensive sex education also cuts across party lines. In a poll of 1,000 self-identified Republicans and Independents, 60 percent of Republicans and 81 percent of Independents think that public schools should teach comprehensive sex education.

Young People Need Comprehensive Sex Education

The health and future of every adolescent is shadowed by risk of sexually transmitted infections (STIs), including HIV, as well as by risk of involvement in unintended pregnancy.

- The rate of STIs is high among young people in the United States. Young people ages 15–24 contract almost half the nation's 19 million new STIs every year; and the CDC [Centers for Disease Control and Prevention] estimates that one in four young women ages 15–19 has an STI.

- Experts estimate that about one young person in the United States is infected with HIV every hour of every day.

- Nearly 15 percent of the 56,000 annual new cases of HIV infections in the United States occurred in youth ages 13 through 24 in 2006.

- African American and Hispanic youth are disproportionately affected by the HIV and AIDS pandemic. Although only 17 percent of the adolescent population in the United States is African American, these teens experienced 69 percent of new AIDS cases among teens in 2006. Latinos ages 20–24 experienced 23 percent of new AIDS cases in 2006 but represented only 18 percent of U.S. young adults.

41

- A November 2006 study of declining pregnancy rates among teens concluded that the reduction in teen pregnancy between 1995 and 2002 was primarily the result of increased use of contraceptives. However, new data from the Centers for Disease Control and Prevention's National Center for Health Statistics [NCHS] show that teen birth rates are again on the rise.

- The NCHS reports a five percent national increase between 2005 and 2007 in teenage birthrates in the U.S; from 40.5 to 42.5 births per 1,000 young women aged 15–19.

- Approximately one in five teens reports some kind of a abuse in a romantic relationship, with girls who experience dating violence having sex earlier than their peers, less likely to use to birth control and more likely to engage in a wide variety of high-risk behaviors.

Research clearly shows that comprehensive sex education programs do not encourage teens to start having sexual intercourse; do not increase the frequency with which teens have intercourse; and do not increase the number of a teen's sexual partners. At the same time, evaluations of publicly funded abstinence-only programs have repeatedly shown no positive changes in sexual behaviors over time. Young people need honest, effective sex education—not ineffective, shame-based abstinence-only programs.

Abstinence Education Is to Blame for Rising Teen Birth Rates

Contraceptive Technology Update

Contraceptive Technology Update *provides objective analysis of the latest research and news on existing and emerging contraceptives.*

Strides in lowering teen pregnancy rates have been reversed. The latest report from Centers for Disease Control and Prevention's National Center for Health Statistics shows that the teen birth rate increased in more than half of all 50 states in 2006, reversing a 14-year drop in numbers. About two-thirds of the increase is attributed to teens ages 18–19, with one-third to teens ages 15–17.

Teen Birth Rates

Nationally, the U.S. teen rate increased from 40.5 births per 1,000 women ages 15–19 in 2005 to 41.9 in 2006. Mississippi, with 68.4 births per 1,000 teen girls ages 15–19, recorded the highest teen birth rate, followed by New Mexico (64.1) and Texas (63.1). Teen birth rates in 2006 were lowest in the Northeast, led by New Hampshire (18.7), Vermont (20.8), and Massachusetts (21.3). The only states with a decrease in teen birth rates between 2005 and 2006 were North Dakota (26.5), Rhode Island (27.8), and New York (25.7).

"It may be that one of the nation's most extraordinary success stories of the past two decades is coming to a close," says Sarah Brown, CEO [chief executive officer] of The National Campaign to Prevent Teen and Unplanned Pregnancy in Washington, DC. "Although teen pregnancy and birth rates have declined by about one-third since the early 1990s, many recent signs, including trends in teen sex and contraceptive use, seemed to have stalled or perhaps gone in the wrong direction."

The federal government's emphasis on abstinence education has left teens without the information they need to make responsible decisions about contraception.

Take a Closer Look

A review of the new data gives further insight into women's health trends:

- A total of 4.3 million births were registered in the United States in 2006, a 3% increase over 2005. The birth rate was 14.2 live births per 1,000 people in 2006, also representing an increase from 2005.

- The average age of mothers giving birth for the first time decreased from 25.2 in 2005 to 25 years in 2006, the first decline in age since the measure became available. The average age at first birth had increased 3.8 years from 1970 to 2003.

- The birth rate for unmarried women increased 7% between 2005 and 2006. There were 50.6 births per 1,000 unmarried women ages 15–44.

- Women were less likely to receive timely prenatal care in 2006. Prenatal care utilization rose steadily from 1990 to 2003, but it remained flat in 2004 and 2005.

- The low birth weight rate (defined as less than 5.5 pounds) rose to 8.3% in 2006, the highest level in four decades. The preterm birth rate also rose in 2006, to 12.8% of all births.

According to an analysis of the 2006 statistics by Child Trends, a Washington, DC-based research group, birth rates per 1,000 females ages 15–19 among Hispanic teens (83) were higher than rates among non-Hispanic black teens (63.7), American Indian teens (54.7), non-Hispanic white teens (26.6), and Asian teens (16.7).

According to the analysis, Hispanic teens represent an important risk group because they are part of the fastest-growing segment of the population. Research indicates that sexually experienced Hispanic adolescents are less likely than other teens to talk to their partners about contraception before sex and to use contraception.

The group that promised to remain abstinent was significantly less likely to use birth control, especially condoms, when they did have sex.

Abstinence Education

Why the rise in teen births? It might be that the federal government's emphasis on abstinence education has left teens without the information they need to make responsible decisions about contraception, Brown observes.

Abstinence-only sex education programs are required to present only the benefits of abstinence to adolescents, so students end up learning one-sided and sometimes incorrect information about condoms and birth control, says Janet Rosenbaum, PhD, a postdoctoral fellow at the Johns Hopkins Bloomberg School of Public Health and the Johns Hopkins STD [sexually transmitted disease] Center in Baltimore. Rosenbaum recently published results of a study that compared teens who took an abstinence pledge with teens of similar backgrounds and beliefs who did not. Findings indicated no difference in pledgers'/nonpledgers' sexual behavior, the age at which they began having sex, or the number of partners; however, the group that promised to remain abstinent was significantly less likely to use birth control, especially condoms, when they did have sex.

A 2004 review found incorrect information in 11 of 13 federally funded abstinence programs, with most of the incorrect material surrounding birth control and condom effectiveness.

More than 90% of abstinence funding does not require that curricula be scientifically accurate. A 2004 review found incorrect information in 11 of 13 federally funded abstinence programs, with most of the incorrect material surrounding birth control and condom effectiveness. Despite those findings, the U.S. government allotted $176 million in FY [fiscal year] 2008 to support programs that exclusively promote abstinence-only behavior outside of marriage.

Abstinence-only programs are not allowed to mention the ways in which condoms protect against disease, only that they do not protect fully against all diseases, Rosenbaum notes. Commonly used abstinence-only curricula do not provide complete, current, or accurate medical knowledge about the effectiveness of condoms, confirms a 2008 review of programs.

Comprehensive Sex Education

Can comprehensive sex education programs make a difference? A 2008 assessment of 56 education programs indicates abstinence-only programs do not delay initiation of sex. However, most comprehensive programs, which emphasize abstinence and the use of protection for those who do have sex, showed strong evidence of positive influence on teens' sexual behavior, including delaying initiation of sex and increasing condom and contraceptive use.

Complacency might have become the enemy of progress when it comes to teen pregnancy, says Brown. Fourteen consecutive years of declines in the teen birth rate might have led to a "ho-hum" view of the issue and diverted important attention, resources, and funding to other pressing issues, she states.

"Let's hope this sobering news on teen births serves as a wake-up call to policy-makers, parents, and practitioners that all our efforts to convince young people to delay pregnancy and parenthood need to be more intense, more creative, and based more on what we know works," says Brown.

Increased funding for teens in need might be harder to get. The Medicaid Family Planning State Option was dropped from the recently implemented federal economic stimulus bill. The option would have allowed states to expand their Medicaid family planning services without having to go through the burdensome Medicaid waiver process. Teens use publicly funded programs; adolescents represent about one in four (28%) contraceptive clients served by publicly supported clinics.

Sex Education Programs Focusing on Virginity Pledges Fail to Reduce Rates of Teen Pregnancy

Dudley Barlow

Dudley Barlow is a retired English teacher with Plymouth Canton High School in Canton, Michigan.

Some years ago, I saw a TV news story about an adolescent girl—in Texas, as I recall—taking a virginity pledge. Could it have been Shelby Knox, the girl who, when she became alarmed about the number of pregnant girls she saw in her high school, changed from being an abstinence only adherent to a sex education reformer? In this ceremony, her father placed a purity ring on her ring finger, and she promised him that she would remain chaste until she married. I thought it was unsettling—creepy really—that in a ceremony emulating a wedding, she would pledge her troth to her dad. If she had premarital sex, it would signal her betrayal of her father? It sounded a little incestuous to me.

Effectiveness of Virginity Pledges

And now, as it turns, we have more substantive reasons to question the value of teenagers taking virginity pledges. They don't work. Harvard researcher Janet Elise Rosenbaum reported on February 13, 2008, in a paper titled "Patient Teenagers?: A Comparison of the Sexual Behavior of Virginity Pledgers and Matched Nonpledgers" that "Virginity pledgers and closely-matched non-pledgers have virtually identical sexual behavior, but pledgers are less likely to protect themselves from pregnancy and disease before marriage than

Dudley Barlow, "Sex Ed. Redux, Redux, Redux," *The Education Digest*, vol. 74, February 2009, pp. 65–68. Reproduced by permission.

matched non-pledgers. Abstinence programs may not affect sexual behavior, but may increase unsafe sex."

In the January 2009 issue of the journal *Pediatrics*, Rosenbaum reported the results of a five-year longitudinal study she conducted on a nationally representative sample of middle and high school students to compare the sexual behavior of students who had taken virginity pledges to the sexual behavior of students who had not taken such pledges.

The results of this study confirmed what she wrote in her February paper. Not only did pledgers and non-pledgers not differ in premarital sex, they had the same incidence and types of sexually transmitted diseases. Pledgers reported 0.1 fewer past-year partners, but did not differ in lifetime sexual partners or the age at which they first had sex. Rosenbaum also reports, curiously enough, that five years after they made virginity pledges, 84% of the pledgers denied ever having pledged.

Pledgers are less likely to protect themselves from pregnancy and disease.

Title V and Sex Education

In "Five Years of Abstinence Only-Until-Marriage Education: Assessing the Impact," Debra Hauser, vice president of Advocates for Youth, reports that: "In 1996, Congress signed into law the Personal Responsibility & Work Opportunities Reconciliation Act, or 'welfare reform.' Attached was the provision, later set out in Section 510(b) of Title V of the Social Security Act, appropriating $250 million dollars over five years for state initiatives promoting sexual abstinence outside of marriage as the only acceptable standard of behavior for young people."

The important point here, of course, is that Title V denies federal funding to any sex education program that does not promote sexual abstinence outside of marriage as the only acceptable standard of behavior for young people. Comprehensive sex education programs, "education that promotes abstinence but includes information about contraception and condoms to build young people's knowledge, attitudes and skills for when they do become sexually active," are not eligible for federal funds.

"For the first five years of the initiative," Hauser reports, "every state but California participated in the program. (California had experimented with its own abstinence-only initiative in the early 1990s. The program was terminated in February 1996, when evaluation results found the program to be ineffective.) From 1998 to 2003, almost a half a billion dollars in state and federal funds were appropriated to support the Title V initiative. A report, detailing the results from the federally funded evaluation of select Title V programs, was due to be released more than a year ago. Last year, Congress extended 'welfare reform' and, with it, the Title V abstinence-only-until-marriage funding without benefit of this, as yet unreleased, report."

Evaluating Abstinence Education

Even though the report on federally funded Title V programs has not been issued, Advocates for Youth did manage to identify evaluations from 10 states. These evaluations measured three things: attitudes endorsing abstinence, intentions to abstain, and actual sexual behavior.

- Four of 10 programs showed increases in attitudes favorable to abstinence. Three of 10 showed mixed results, and 3 had no significant impact on attitudes.

- Three of 9 programs showed a favorable impact on intentions to abstain. Two of 9 showed mixed results, and 4 of 9 showed no significant impact on participants' intentions to abstain.

- Finally, 1 of 6 programs showed mixed results in changes in sexual behavior. Three of 6 programs showed no impact, and 2 of 6 programs actually reported increases in sexual behavior. Possible causes of the increased sexual behavior were unclear.

"Two evaluations," Hauser writes, "—Iowa's and the Pennsylvania Fulton County program compared the impact of comprehensive sex education with that of abstinence-only-until-marriage programs.

"In Iowa, abstinence-only students were slightly more likely than comprehensive sex education participants to feel strongly about wanting to postpone sex, but less likely to feel that their goals should not include teen pregnancy. There was little to no difference between the abstinence-only students and those in the comprehensive sex education program in understanding of why they should wait to have sex. Evaluations did not include comparison of data on the sexual behavior of participants in the two types of programs.

"In Fulton County, PA, results found few to no differences between the abstinence-only and comprehensive approaches in attitudes towards sexual behavior. Evaluators found that, regardless of which program was implemented in the 7th and 8th grades, sexual attitudes, intentions, and behaviors were similar by the end of the 10th grade."

But the bottom line is this: "No evaluation demonstrated any impact on reducing teens' sexual behavior at follow-up, 3 to 17 months after the program ended."

Finally, Hauser reports that the results of these surveys are consistent with other studies that have been done on the efficacy of abstinence-only sex education. She cites the work of researcher Doug Kirby. "In a 1994 review of sex education programs, Kirby et al. assessed all the studies available at the time of school-based, abstinence-only programs that had received peer review and that measured attitudes, intentions, and behavior. Kirby et al. found that none of the three abstinence only programs was effective in producing a statistically significant impact on sexual behaviors in program participants relative to comparisons. In a 1997 report for the National Campaign to Prevent Teen Pregnancy, . . . Kirby reviewed evaluations from six abstinence-only programs, again finding no program that produced a statistically significant change in sexual behavior. This was again confirmed in 2000, when another review by Kirby found no abstinence-only program that produced statistically significant changes in sexual behaviors among program youth relative to comparisons."

Evaluators noted more than once that the programs' emphasis on the failure rates of contraception, including condoms, left youth ambivalent, at best, about using them.

Hauser also writes that a few of the evaluators of the 10 state programs were concerned that abstinence-only programs failed to address the needs of the significant number of sexually active youth.

The concerned evaluators remarked that abstinence-only programs failed to provide youth with information they needed to protect themselves from pregnancy and sexually transmitted diseases.

Ironically, abstinence-only programs may actually increase these risks for sexually active teens. Hauser writes, "Evaluators noted more than once that the programs' emphasis on the failure rates of contraception, including condoms, left youth ambivalent, at best, about using them." One wonders whether an underlying premise of abstinence-only programs is that sexually active youth are beyond the pale and are, therefore, on their own.

The Call for Comprehensive Sex Education

Brian DeVries, of the National Sexuality Resource Center, says, "We want people to know that abstinence-only education doesn't work. Sex educators know. Teens know. Parents know. And the research shows it. When will our policies and interventions reflect what science, research, and best practices demonstrate? We need comprehensive sexuality education that is truly comprehensive."

Abstinence-only education is dangerous for students who simply are not abstaining.

The federal government spends about $200 million annually on abstinence programs that are demonstrably ineffective, but it is difficult to imagine that members of Congress will be in a hurry to curtail funding for these programs. Who among them (particularly members from conservative areas of the country) is likely to risk being labeled as someone who wants to encourage premarital sex?

So, are we stuck with this impassable divide between social conservatives who believe in abstinence-only sex education and social liberals who promote comprehensive sex education? Perhaps not. In an article titled "Red Sex, Blue Sex" in the November 3, 2008, *New Yorker*, Margaret Talbot holds out some hope for a view that might help to bridge this divide. She says Shelby Knox "occupies a middle ground. She testified [at a congressional hearing] that it's possible to 'believe in abstinence in a religious sense,' but still understand that abstinence-only education is dangerous for students who simply are not abstaining.

"As Knox's approach makes clear, . . . you can encourage teenagers to postpone sex for all kinds of practical, emotional, and moral reasons. A new 'abstinence-plus' curriculum, now growing in popularity, urges abstinence while providing accurate information about contraception and reproduction for those who have sex anyway. 'Abstinence works,' Knox said. 'Abstinence-only-until-marriage does not.'"

Sex Education in Schools Does Not Reduce Rates of Teen Pregnancy

Michael Castleman

Michael Castleman has written about sexuality since 1974. Currently he publishes GreatSexAfter40.com, which focuses on love-making in the second half of life, but answers sexuality questions from people of all ages.

Everyone wants fewer teen pregnancies and fewer cases of sexually transmitted diseases (STDs). The question is: How do we get there?

Conservatives demand that school sex education programs be limited to promotion of abstinence until marriage. Liberals insist on lessons about all the contraceptives, and STD prevention, which means promotion of condoms. The two sides appear to be passionately antagonistic. But that's an illusion. Actually, they share remarkably similar core values. And neither of their approaches has been shown to reduce teen sex, pregnancies, or STDs.

Meanwhile, a large body of research reveals the real key to reducing teen sexual irresponsibility: parents' willingness to discuss their sexual values with their kids. If schools jettisoned sex education classes and instead sponsored seminars to help parents become better sex educators at home, it's clear that teen pregnancies and STDs would decline. Parents also might encourage teen sexual responsibility based on a concept foreign to both liberals and conservatives, the simple fact that safe sex is better sex.

The Truth About Teens and Sex

Both liberals and conservatives rail about "the teen sex crisis." Hence the political tug-of-war over sex education in schools. If there ever was a teen sex crisis, it has abated. Over the past 15 years, surveys by the federal Centers for Disease Control and Prevention (CDC) show that teens have become considerably more conservative and responsible. From 1991 to 2003:

- Teens reporting intercourse dropped from 54 percent to 47 percent.

- Among sexually active teens, condom use jumped from 46 percent to 63 percent.

- Births to teens fell 33 percent.

- Teen diagnoses of the most prevalent STD, chlamydia, have remained roughly the same for the past 10 years.

Conservatives insist the decline in teen sex proves that abstinence education is paying off. They are mistaken. The abstinence push began in 1998. But according to the CDC, teen STD (chlamydia) rates have not changed significantly in ten years. The teen birth rate started falling seven years earlier. Abstinence-only sex ed is most deeply entrenched in the South, and notably less popular in the rest of the country. Guess where teens are most likely to become pregnant—in the South. According to the CDC, teen birth rates in Alabama, Mississippi, and South Carolina are two to three times those in Vermont, New York, and Minnesota. Abstinence programs ask teens to vow virginity until marriage. But a CDC study shows that only 12 percent of those who take virginity vows keep them. In other words, abstinence education has an 88 percent failure rate. Finally, researchers at McMaster University in Hamilton, Ontario, analyzed 26 studies of efforts to reduce teen pregnancy. Abstinence-only programs did not delay first intercourse. In fact, pregnancies often increased.

I hate to say it, but liberal sex education fares no better. Before I became a journalist, I worked in family planning. I talked up contraceptives and STD prevention in many middle schools and high schools. I thought I got through to the students. I was mistaken. The McMaster analysis included many liberal programs. They, too, had no impact: no delay of intercourse, no increased use of contraceptives, and no fewer pregnancies.

If neither conservatives nor liberals deserve credit for the 15-year decline in teen sex, who does? Parents. They have been discussing sex with their children—and getting through to them.

"Dangers-of-Sex" Education

Where I live, San Francisco, the liberal sex education program includes STD prevention and all the contraceptives. Nonetheless, my son came home and announced that only one contraceptive is 100 percent effective—abstinence.

Nonsense. Another method is 100 percent effective—not to mention, popular, enjoyable, and free. It's non-intercourse lovemaking, genital massage, and oral sex. But even the most liberal programs never mention it. To do so would acknowledge sexual pleasure, and negate the core value that unites liberals and conservatives more than anything divides them, namely, that for teens, sex is dangerous. Forget "sex education." What schools provide is "dangers-of-sex" education.

The Answer: Parents Talking About Sex

If neither conservatives nor liberals deserve credit for the 15-year decline in teen sex, who does? Parents. They have been discussing sex with their children—and getting through to them.

Now I happen to be the father of two teens, both great kids, but do they listen to me? Rarely. As a result, it's been hard for me to believe that parents actually get through to kids about sex.

Parents get through. A great deal of research consistently shows that when parents discuss sex, teens delay it, and, when teens become sexual, they're much more likely to use condoms. The most compelling evidence comes from a CDC survey. Compared with teens whose mothers did not discuss condoms, those whose moms did were three times more likely to use condoms during their first sexual experience and those who did were 20 times more likely to use them subsequently.

Sex educators moan that parents are uncomfortable discussing sex, refuse to do so, and are often misinformed. Hence sex education in schools. I contend that to be effective sex educators, parents need not be comfortable, eloquent, or erudite. All they have to do is try.

Parents are trying—even if they don't want to. AIDS forced it on them. AIDS was identified in 1981 but wasn't widely perceived as a threat to heterosexuals until about a decade later—until the early 1990s, when the teen sex rate began its steady decline and teen condom use began increasing.

School sex education programs have no impact on teens. In other words, they're a waste of money. They should be abolished.

Welcome to Sex Ed Class—for Parents

School sex education programs have no impact on teens. In other words, they're a waste of money. They should be abolished. Instead, schools should invest their sex education dollars in another group. They should offer classes to parents to help them discuss sex with their children. Conservatives argue that sex education belongs in the home because it involves values, something parents should teach. They're right—not just because parents control the message but because home-based sex education actually works.

Could parent-empowerment classes work? The research is scant, but Penn State researchers offered mothers of teens two brief classes on discussing sexual issues. Afterward, their children said it was easier to talk about sex with their moms, and the mothers and teens spent more time discussing sexual issues.

If conservative parents want to demand abstinence until marriage, that's their prerogative. But my wife and I have taken a different tack with our kids. We promote consent, condoms, lubrication, and sexual pleasure.

Consent. No coercion ever. If you feel coerced, do whatever is necessary to extricate yourself from the situation. We'll help if it's at all possible.

Condoms. When used carefully, condoms virtually eliminate pregnancy and STD risk. Conservatives overestimate condom failure rates. As contraceptives, condoms are 85 to 98 percent effective. This does not mean 2 to 15 pregnancies per 100 acts of condom-covered intercourse. It means that if 100 couples use condoms exclusively for a year, 2 to 15 can expect an accidental pregnancy. That's pretty effective. The fact is, when condoms are used carefully, they're almost as effective as the Pill. Overall, they're better than the Pill because they also prevent STDs, including AIDS.

Lubrication. Vaginal lubrication reduces the risk of condom breakage. In addition, adequate lubrication increases comfort during intercourse. Many women don't produce much natural lubrication, especially teenage girls anxious about sex. Commercial lubricants are inexpensive, take only a few seconds to apply, and greatly enhance sexual comfort. When our son became sexually active, we gave him and his girlfriend a vial of lubricant. They thanked us.

Sexual pleasure. The most enjoyable sex is based not on lust but on trust and relaxation. Who can trust a lover who ignores the risks of pregnancy and STDs? Safe sex is more than public health hype. It's crucial to the deep relaxation necessary to give and receive sexual pleasure.

This country sells everything with sex. Why not use sexual pleasure to sell sexual responsibility? It's one of the few places where a "sex sell" is actually appropriate.

My wife and I have told our two teens: When you feel ready for partner sex, embrace sexual responsibility, because it leads to better sex. A radical notion, perhaps. But I believe our approach might further reduce teen pregnancy and STDs. It might also help teens grow up to be something they all truly want to be—good lovers.

CHAPTER 2

Does Pop Culture Contribute to Teen Pregnancy?

Chapter Preface

According to Monitoring the Future, in 2005 "Three out of every four students (75%) have consumed alcohol (more than just a few sips) by the end of high school. . . . Half of teens (50%) have tried an illicit drug by the time they finish high school." The trend of alcohol and drug use among teens is cause for concern. And teens who use drugs and alcohol tend to be more sexually active than their peers, increasing their risk of pregnancy.

According to the National Campaign to Prevent Teen Pregnancy, "50 percent of teens say drinking and drugs are the main reason teens don't use contraception when they have sex." When under the influence of alcohol and drugs, a person's judgment is impaired, which can lead to unplanned and unprotected sex. Teens report having unprotected sex because they were caught up in the moment and did not have contraception readily available, or they forgot to use it. Having spontaneous sex while under the influence can lead to regret and feelings of guilt. Teens report losing their virginity or having sex with someone they would not become involved with sexually when sober.

When under the influence of alcohol and drugs, teens also are at an increased risk for date rape. Date rape is when a person is forced to have sex against her or his will by a friend or acquaintance. It is never okay for a person to force him or herself onto somebody. If a person is forced to perform a sexual act by someone else, the person being forced is not at fault, even if he or she was under the influence of drugs or alcohol at the time of the incident. Victims of date rape need to report the incident to police and seek prompt medical attention. Alcohol consumption also increases a person's risk of unknowingly being slipped date rape drugs, such as so-called roofies or GHB (gamma hydroxy butyrate), in drinks. These drugs can cause lack of memory, blackouts, and even death. Furthermore, an unexpected pregnancy can result from date rape.

If a teen has drug and alcohol dependency, an intervention involving substance abuse counseling may be necessary. Pregnant teens struggling with drug and alcohol dependency risk giving birth to babies who have low birth weight, birth defects, mental retardation, and fetal alcohol syndrome. Falling into the sex, drugs, and rock-and-roll lifestyle at a young age can have lifelong consequences, which affect not only the teens but also their families and communities. For example, substance abuse can lead not only to unplanned pregnancy but also expulsion from school, an unfavorable reputation, denial of college loans, and a criminal record. Parents and guardians can help teens avoid the pitfalls of alcohol and drug use by keeping the lines of communication open. Teens who are actively involved in sports, volunteer work, hobbies, and other extracurricular activities are less likely to use drugs and alcohol and are less likely to experience unplanned pregnancy. The viewpoints in the following chapter further explore the influence pop culture has on teen pregnancy and parenting.

Sex on Television Contributes to Teen Pregnancy

Rob Stein

Rob Stein is a staff writer for the Washington Post *who focuses on health and medicine.*

Teenagers who watch a lot of television featuring flirting, necking, discussion of sex and sex scenes are much more likely than their peers to get pregnant or get a partner pregnant, according to the first study to directly link steamy programming to teen pregnancy.

The study, which tracked more than 700 12- to 17-year-olds for three years, found that those who viewed the most sexual content on TV were about twice as likely to be involved in a pregnancy as those who saw the least.

"Watching this kind of sexual content on television is a powerful factor in increasing the likelihood of a teen pregnancy," said lead researcher Anita Chandra. "We found a strong association."

The study is being published today in *Pediatrics*, the journal of the American Academy of Pediatrics.

Teen Pregnancy Rates

There is rising concern about teen pregnancy rates, which after decades of decline may have started inching up again, fuelling an intense debate about what factors are to blame.

Although TV viewing is unlikely to entirely explain the possible uptick in teen pregnancies, Chandra and others said, the study provides the first direct evidence that it could be playing a significant role.

"Sexual content on television has doubled in the last few years, especially during the period of our research," said Chandra, a researcher at the non-partisan Rand Corp. in the United States.

Studies have found a link between watching television shows with sexual content and becoming sexually active earlier.

"The television content we see very rarely highlights the negative aspects of sex or the risks and responsibilities," Chandra said. "So if teens are getting any information about sex, they're rarely getting information about pregnancy or sexually transmitted diseases."

Studies have found a link between watching television shows with sexual content and becoming sexually active earlier, and between sexually explicit music videos and an increased risk of sexually transmitted diseases. And many studies have shown that TV violence seems to make children more aggressive. But the new research is the first to show an association between TV watching and pregnancy among teens.

The study did not examine how different approaches to sex education factor into the effects of TV viewing on sexual behaviour and pregnancy rates. Proponents of comprehensive sex education, as well as programs that focus on abstinence, said the findings illustrate the need to educate children better about the risks of sex and about how to protect themselves, although they disagree about which approach works best.

"We have a highly sexualized culture that glamourizes sex," said Valerie Huber of the National Abstinence Education Association. "We really need to encourage schools to make abstinence-centred programs a priority."

But others said there is no evidence that abstinence-centred programs work.

"This finding underscores the importance of evidence-based sex education that helps young people delay sex and use prevention when they become sexually active," said James Wagoner of Advocates for Youth. "The absolutely last thing we should do in response is bury our heads in the sand and promote failed abstinence-only programs."

The likelihood of getting pregnant or getting someone else pregnant increased steadily with the amount of sexual content they watched on TV.

Viewing Sexual Content and Teen Pregnancy

Chandra and her colleagues surveyed more than 2,000 adolescents ages 12 to 17 three times by telephone from 2001 to 2004 to gather information about a variety of behavioural and demographic factors, including television viewing habits. Based on a detailed analysis of the sexual content of 23 shows in the 2000–01 TV season, the researchers calculated how often the teens saw characters kissing, touching, having sex and discussing past or future sexual activity.

Among the 718 youths who reported being sexually active during the study, the likelihood of getting pregnant or getting someone else pregnant increased steadily with the amount of sexual content they watched on TV, the researchers found. About 25 per cent of those who watched the most were involved in a pregnancy, compared with about 12 per cent of those who watched the least. The researchers took into account other factors such as having only one parent, wanting to have a baby and engaging in other risky behaviours.

Fifty-eight girls reported getting pregnant and 33 boys reported being responsible for getting a girl pregnant during the study period. The increased risk emerged regardless of whether teens watched only one or two shows that were explicit or surfed many shows that had occasional sexual content, Chandra said.

"It could be a child wasn't watching that much TV per week but was watching shows that got a pretty high rating on sexual content, or it could be a kid who was watching a lot of hours but on average was getting just moderate amounts of sexual content from each show," Chandra said.

Among the shows the teens watched were *Sex and the City*, *Friends* and *That '70s Show*. Chandra would not identify the others but stressed that they included dramas, comedies, reality shows and even animated programs on broadcast and cable networks.

"We don't want to single out any individual programs," Chandra said.

The researchers recommended that parents spend more time monitoring what their children watch and discussing what they see, including pointing out the possible negative consequences of early sexual activity. Programmers should also include more-realistic portrayals of the risks of sex, such as sexually transmitted diseases and pregnancy, the researchers said.

"Unfortunately, that continues to be relatively rare compared to the portrayals of the positive aspects," Chandra said.

Teen Pregnancy and the Media's Role

Critics of television programming and experts on teen pregnancy said the research provided powerful new evidence about the role of TV in youth behaviour.

"This is very significant," said Melissa Henson of the Parents Television Council, a watchdog group. "It gives us plenty of reason for concern."

Kelleen Kaye of the National Campaign to Prevent Teen and Unplanned Pregnancy praised the study but stressed that the causes of teen pregnancy are complex.

"We need to be cautious about overreaching in our expectations about the role the media can play in our effort to prevent teen pregnancy," she said. "We don't want to assume this is the whole story."

Several experts questioned whether the study had established a causal relationship.

"It may be the kids who have an interest in sex watch shows with sexual content," said Laura Lindberg of the Guttmacher Institute. "I'm concerned this makes it seem like if we just shut off the TV we'd dramatically reduce the teen pregnancy rate."

Chandra acknowledged that other factors might play a role but said the findings are compelling because the researchers were able to track the teens over time and found such a striking relationship.

"The magnitude of the association we did see was very strong," she said.

A second study in *Pediatrics* adds to existing evidence that youths who play violent video games—a worldwide trend with American children averaging 13 hours of video gaming a week—led to increased physically aggressive behaviour.

Researchers from the United States and Japan evaluated more than 1,200 Japanese youths and 364 Americans between nine and 18 years old and found a "significant risk factor for later physically aggressive behaviour . . . across very different cultures."

Parents Do Matter

Stephan Dunay

Stephan Dunay is a staff writer for Sex, Etc., *a Web site and national magazine that provides sexuality education information to young people and adults.*

Many teens today would attempt some of the disgusting stunts seen on *Fear Factor* before admitting they want a closer, more open relationship with their parents. Our rebellious teen instinct tells us it's OK to love our parents, but not show it or act like we need them.

So, we push them aside and pretend that we can make it on our own, but who are we kidding? Growing up is much more difficult without the aid and advice of a parent or guardian.

Many teens act like they don't want their parents to care, but according to Bill Albert, communications director for the National Campaign to Prevent Teen Pregnancy in Washington, D.C., many "wish that their parents were more deeply involved in their lives."

Albert says that when it comes to schoolwork, social interaction and issues like sex and drugs, "young people benefit from close relationships with adults. It is unfair and unwise to leave young people without adult guidance and supervision."

After all, the teen years are some of the most difficult ones we face, and it is nearly impossible for me to imagine going through so much change and pressure without some adult guidance and mentoring. This is especially true when it comes to sexual health issues.

Stephan Dunay, "Parents Do Matter," *Sex, Etc.* September 4, 2008. Reprinted with permission from Sex, Etc., the national magazine and Web site written by teens, for teens, published by Answer at Rutgers, The State University of New Jersey. http://sexetc.org.

Teens, Sex, and the Media

As teens, we're exposed daily to mixed signals and subliminal messages that distort our perceptions of sex, drugs, and violence. Images of Britney Spears making out with Madonna at the MTV VMA's [Music Television's Video Music Awards] and listening to Nelly singing about "shakin' yer tail feather" can stick with us for a long time.

A world of propaganda surrounds us, attempting to suck us into a world of sex, drugs, and rock-n-roll.

And these messages are everywhere. Radio, television, movies, newspapers, magazines, billboards, friends. A world of propaganda surrounds us, attempting to suck us into a world of sex, drugs, and rock-n-roll. Although the media portray things that look like a lot of fun, some of these things are very dangerous and could end up destroying your life.

The media can leave a teen confused. That's where the adults come in. They can often help us sort out these extremely exaggerated images and answer our questions about sex, drugs, and violence. Without an adult to help, it's difficult to tell the difference between right and wrong and the "media world" versus the "real world."

Plenty of teens back this up. According to a recent poll conducted by the National Campaign to Prevent Teen Pregnancy, 88 percent of 12- to 21-year-olds say it would be easier to postpone sexual activity if they could have more open, honest conversations about these topics with their parents.

Open Communication

Talking to parents gives teens more information and a better understanding of themselves and the choices they face. Parents should talk to their adolescents about the risks involved with sexual activity, forms of protection, and the benefits of remaining abstinent. When that happens, teens make better choices.

"My parents are really understanding, and I feel very comfortable talking to them about a lot of stuff," says Dana, 17, of Pennington, NJ. "They definitely have helped me decide to wait for sex."

The sad part is that too many parents and teens never talk about this stuff. According to the Campaign's survey, 23 percent of respondents said they have never discussed sex, contraception, or pregnancy with their parents.

"I just don't have any time to [talk to my parents]," says 18-year-old Chris, also of Pennington. "I'm never home when they are and they're never home when I am. We hardly even have dinner together."

So . . . maybe it's not all the parents' fault? Students are spending less time at home and it should be partially teens' responsibility to approach their parents with questions or concerns. Yeah, like that would ever happen. Many teens would never admit that they need advice from their parents.

So, what do we do? First, we have to overcome the disconnection between kids and parents.

A lot of parents want to be involved. We just send tons of signals that say, "Stand back."

Initiating Communication

Another Campaign survey conducted in 2003 found that 45 percent of teens say parents are the most influential people in their lives. The problem is that parents don't know it. Forty-eight percent of parents think their teens are more influenced by their friends.

So, maybe we should tell them the truth. Maybe we should let them know that we're more likely to either wait to have sex or have safer sex, if they talk to us. Maybe we should tell them that we're less likely to get involved with drugs or alcohol, if they talk to us.

Maybe, when they ask us, "How was school today?" we should give them some details and not just shrug and say, "OK." A lot of parents want to be involved. We just send tons of signals that say, "Stand back."

Questions are a great way to get the conversation started. Parents were teenagers once, too (hard to believe, I know). A lot of them drank and experimented with drugs and sex. They may actually know a few things.

So, speak up, ask questions, and learn from your parents. Don't put all of the responsibility on them to talk. Spark up a conversation with something as simple as the latest school gossip or weekend plans and work your way into the more sensitive questions and concerns.

Some guys and girls may ask, "Well, what if I only have one parent?" This, unfortunately, is a tougher situation if you are a guy being raised by a single mom or a girl being raised by a single dad. Talk to your parent anyway. If he or she doesn't have the answers, go with him or her to the library or bookstore or even try to find the answers on the Internet with them.

Tell your parent to check out this Web site called *Talking with Kids*. It gives tips on how to answer teens' questions without making the situation uncomfortable. This may be easier said than done, but these types of Q & A [question and answer] sessions with your parents will end up being a rewarding learning and bonding experience for the both of you.

Your parents will either have or will search out solid answers to your questions because they care about you and want you to live a healthy and successful life. These conversations will most likely lead to a more comfortable and friendly relationship between you. You may even end up finding things out about them that you never knew.

Popular Media Glamorize Teen Pregnancy

Brian Housman

Brian Housman, a writer and speaker to parents and teens, is the author of Engaging Your Teen's World. *He also is director of the nonprofit Awake to Life.*

2008 has shaped up to be the year of the pregnant teen. Whether from a fashion mag, gossip blog, or respectable news source, it seems that every other week there has been headline news on the issue. That more than a million teen girls get pregnant each year is a given. The difference this year has been the response from the public. It has been either a cutesy fascination or a wide-eyed shock that lasts no longer than a hiccup.

Early on in the year we saw *Juno*, starring newcomer Ellen Page, win an Academy Award. The film is about a teen girl who gets pregnant after having sex with her best friend just so they could both know what sex is like. Despite the fact the film skirts the "friends with benefits" issue, you still found yourself rooting for the spunky Juno who deals with pregnancy in a disarming and responsible manner. Another unexpected hit a few months earlier was the crude comedy *Knocked Up* about a twenty-something single who gets pregnant after a drunken one night stand. Both films showed some of the consequences of the pregnancies, but also come to an end like a nice little package with a bow on top.

Shortly after, *Time* magazine coined the phrase "The Juno Effect" when scores of teen girls began to talk about how much fun it would be to have a baby of their own. Then we heard that a group of seventeen Massachusetts girls formed a

Brian Housman, "Teen Pregnancy Not All Happy Smiles," Awake to Life, 2008. Reproduced by permission.

pact to get pregnant together. Some of the girls even reported to be disappointed when they found out they weren't pregnant.

Instead of the full picture, all we see is the cute baby and the celebrity mom.

While all this was happening, tabloids and teen mags were running constant photos and tidbits on Nicole Richie's and Jamie Lynn Spears' "baby bumps." Each photo showed an excited young celeb waving to an eager public more interested in the future babies' names than how the mothers-to-be were dealing with the reality that every part of their young lives were about to change.

Suddenly being a teen mother has become cool.

There has been the usual initial shock from parents but it has been fleeting. It's almost like parents too have gotten desensitized. It's become just a normal part of what they expect from teenagers. Typically when something becomes a hot topic, parents take to the streets. Whether it's drinking and driving, school violence, or gangs, parents are always ready to take action. But not so with this. It's been more of a whimper.

Figuring It Out Along the Way

As a result, teens are left to filter the movies and media on their own. In an interview with NPR [National Public Radio], Jane Brown from the *Teen Media Project* said, "It is unusual that we would be glamorizing pregnant celebrities, and we don't even know who the fathers are. . . ." But that's where we are now. Instead of the full picture, all we see is the cute baby and a celebrity mom whose body snaps back to normal in a few weeks.

No one mentions that movie moms were merely actors who've gone on to their next role. No one mentions that the teen celeb with a baby also has several nannies, a publicist, housekeepers, servants, and more. All the average teen mom has is herself. No one mentions the cost of the nutritionists, weight coaches, and gym instructors who helped celebs lose the pregnancy weight. And definitely, no one mentions the loss of personal time, loss of potential, and loss of friendships that are likely to result. Instead, in the end, Juno remains best friends with the boy and all goes back to normal.

Maybe even in real-life-Hollywood it's not that simple. Just this week there was a sad update on Jamie Lynn Spears' personal life. *InTouch* magazine confirmed that her fiance, Casey Aldridge, continued to have a sexual relationship with another woman while Jamie Lynn was pregnant. I wonder though if the news will get anything more than a yawn from the teen audience.

Hollywood Takes Another Swing at It

Even with its shortcomings, *Juno* was a well done movie. It was great seeing Juno take responsibility for her actions and show maturity in giving the baby up for adoption, but I'm still waiting for someone to show the whole picture. Recent attempts from Hollywood to deal with the issue on a broader scale are getting closer than before.

ABC Family struck gold with the summer's biggest cable hit, *The Secret Life of the American Teen*, about a family whose young daughter gets pregnant. Though a teen soap, it features parents who are not completely out of touch and a young mother-to-be who is already experiencing some of the social consequences that come with being pregnant at school. The National Campaign to Prevent Teen and Unplanned Pregnancy has even created weekly Episode Discussion Guides that can be downloaded.

Not to be outdone, NBC has been running *The Baby Borrowers*, a reality show with five teen couples who learn what it's like to be parents. Much like *Secret Life*, *Baby Borrowers* isn't showing a glassy-eyed view of teen parenthood but rather the struggles to live a new identity and learn to deal with sleeplessness, self-control, and sacrifice.

Even with Hollywood doing a better job hitting the mark, this still doesn't give parents a free pass. We must move into the broken parts of adolescent culture to speak truth and share the freedom that comes with sex being experienced within God's design. We must get past the awkwardness of having a conversation with teens (at younger ages) about a once-taboo subject. Perhaps most difficult for some of us, we must be willing to be transparent with our kids when talking about our own sexual choices in the past, lest they find themselves moving toward the same poor choices.

Teens Use Technology to Obtain Factual Information About Sex and Pregnancy

Tim Weldon

Tim Weldon works at The Council of State Governments as an education policy analyst.

The text comes in: *I'm 14 and am going to lose my virginity but am not on birth control. Am I at high risk for pregnancy?*

The response: *Yes. A sexually active teen who does not use birth control has a 90% chance of becoming pregnant within a year. You need to use protection. Even if you don't become pregnant you are still at risk of an STD* [sexually transmitted disease].

This actual interchange is an example of information provided through the Birds and Bees Text Line, funded by the state of North Carolina. Teens can text a question about sexuality and get an answer, usually within 24 hours. The phone numbers are deleted and the entire process is anonymous.

New Media

Communicating information about sexual relationships, pregnancy and sexually transmitted diseases has come a long way from the days when teenagers learned about those topics through sex education textbooks or pamphlets in school, or, if they were fortunate, through face-to-face conversations with their parents in their living rooms after dinner.

Even the more recent and increasingly graphic sexual health information published in teen magazines or broadcast on television networks appear to be passé. Now, a growing

Tim Weldon, "Sex and the New Media," *State News*, August 2009, pp. 17–19. Copyright © 2009 The Council of State Governments. Reproduced with permission.

number of teenagers send and receive text messages by the dozens, belong to multiple online social networking sites, and use blogs, widgets and Twitter, which have only recently joined the lexicon of tech-speak. These media have become new avenues to send or receive sexual information.

As teenagers turn to these digital sources of information—the new media—public health officials are finding a golden opportunity to inform young people about preventing unplanned pregnancy and STDs.

As teenagers turn to digital sources of information—the new media—public health officials are finding a golden opportunity to inform young people about preventing unplanned pregnancy and STDs.

Birds and Bees Texting

In North Carolina, which has one of the nation's highest teen pregnancy rates, the Adolescent Pregnancy Prevention Campaign of North Carolina developed the Birds and the Bees Text Line to answer questions about sex, relationships and STDs. North Carolina's General Assembly earmarked approximately $250,000 for the campaign, and $5,000 of that funding is used to operate the Birds and Bees Text Line.

And the questions are still coming in.

Text question: *Is it legal for a 17-year-old to be with a 14-year-old?*

Text answer: *It is legal but is it a good idea? . . . It's best to stick with someone your own age.*

Text question: *If you have sex under water do you need a condom?*

Text answer: *Yes, use a condom to protect against pregnancy and STDs every time you have sex.*

In its first three months, the Birds and Bees Text Line received approximately 700 questions. Kay Phillips, the line's director, said 11 staff members are trained to provide non-judgmental answers to the queries. "Our purpose is to reduce teen pregnancies and STDs," she said. "The purpose is not to teach kids how to have sex. . . . Our purpose is to help these kids learn and make better decisions."

Pushback from Parents

Phillips acknowledges, however, she has received criticism at meetings throughout North Carolina. That criticism often comes from parents who oppose a program that enables their children to receive information about sex, including contraception, from anonymous staff working for a publicly run program, particularly since North Carolina mandates abstinence-only sex education curriculum in schools.

Sometimes a young person might have a question that they are two frightened to ask their parents.

"I totally agree that (talking about sex) should be done in the home, but the reality of that is that it is not being done in the home," Phillips said. She adds, "If there is an opportunity, we . . . encourage them to talk to their parents. But as you know, not every person out there has a happy family life."

Bill Albert, chief program officer for the National Campaign to Prevent Teen and Unplanned Pregnancy, also known as The National Campaign, agrees information about sex should come from parents. But that doesn't always happen.

"Sometimes a young person might have a question that they are too frightened to ask their parents," Albert said, referring to the Birds and Bees Line, "And they are going to ask somebody, and I'm pleased that a responsible group is trying to answer them."

But Albert also has pointed comments for parents who categorically oppose the use of new media to provide information about sex and relationships to teens.

"I don't understand in this day and age this antiquated notion that a lot of parents have that 'I can shield my kid from topic X.' I think that is almost impossible in this day and age," he said.

The National Campaign launched a Web site for teenagers that provides information about sex, pregnancy, relationships and STDs. During May 2009, the Web site, *www.stayteen.org*, included situational quiz questions. More than 400,000 people participated. The Web site also operates a widget, which can be embedded in a teenager's social networking site, such as Myspace or Facebook, to provide them with a link to credible sexual information every time they use their social networking pages.

The National Campaign's Web site also allows young people to ask nonmedical questions about sex and relationships. Albert points out one of the values of Web 2.0—the term used to apply to the new generation of Web development and design—is the interaction it provides, inviting comment and conversation from teenagers about sensitive subjects.

He acknowledged the Internet contains considerable misinformation about sexual health, but he believes *www.stay teen.org* is a way to combat potentially harmful information.

Reaching Teens Where They Are

The problems of teen pregnancy and STDs among adolescents and young adults are well-documented. According to the Centers for Disease Control and Prevention [CDC], after declining steadily between 1991 and 2005, the teen pregnancy rate is again increasing nationally. In 2007, there were 42.5 births per 1,000 females in the 15- to 19-year-old age group. It marked the second consecutive year the teen pregnancy rate increased.

Adolescents and young adults also account for the highest reported rates of two STDs—gonorrhea and chlamydia, according to statistics from the Centers for Disease Control and

Prevention. Young people ages 15 to 24 have five times the reported chlamydia rate and four times the reported gonorrhea rate as the general population, the CDC reports.

Public health officials are discovering that using forms of the media popular with young people—such as cell phones, the Internet and social networking sites—is one way to provide information that might help prevent an unwanted pregnancy or an STD.

Kids go online to get health information, and one of the main topics they're looking for is sex and sexuality.

"We're pretty slow, especially in public health, to get on the bandwagon," admits Rachel Kachur, health communication specialist for the CDC. "And I feel we've done a decent job of figuring out how to be in these spaces, because we have to put accurate, useful information out there in order to compete with all that other stuff that's out there."

Kachur insists that adolescents want information about sexual health, but don't always know where to access reliable and nonjudgemental facts. She believes the new media have the potential to reach many of them.

"Kids go online to get health information, and one of the main topics they're looking for is sex and sexuality," she said. "Kids are using the Internet for health information. . . . It's up to us to provide them with reliable information and credible resources."

Children and adolescents between the ages of 8 and 18 consume an average of 44 hours of media time per week, according to Albert from the National Campaign to Prevent Teen and Unplanned Pregnancy. He points out that's more time than they spend in school and more time than most young people spend with their parents. "Teens are already knee-deep in cyberspace. Why would you not try to reach them there?" he asks.

Kachur believes the use of new media offers young people a way they can "feel normal" about their sexual development.

"When kids are coming into their own sexuality and trying to figure out who they are, they can find others like them online. That's really important when you think back at how difficult it is to be a teenager and trying to fit in," Kachur said.

Other Programs Join the New Media

Deb Levine, executive director of California-based ISIS Inc., a nonprofit organization focused on developing technology for promotion of sexual health and healthy relationships, was instrumental in the creation of GoAskAlice at Columbia University in 1993, believed to be the first Web site where people could anonymously ask questions about sexual health issues. More than 15 years later, she is still encouraging policymakers to embrace technology as a means of providing sexual information to young people.

"The computer and technology is not a panacea," she said. "It works best in combination with other ways of reaching young people. . . . So it's not that this is going to replace other ways that we communicate, but it's a complement to other services that we're providing."

Through a CDC-funded program, the New Media Institute at the University of Georgia led an effort in 2008 for students from seven colleges to produce videos that can be broadcast onto someone's cell phone to fight the spread of HIV. What came from that program is The AIDS Personal Public Service Announcement project, designed to increase awareness of the importance of HIV testing and to encourage young people to get tested.

"They're spending more time on the phone than with any other medium. It's a device that is constantly with them," the institute's director, Scott Shamp, pointed out. "That's where they're going for answers. That's why we need to make sure that those answers are easily available and that they're accurate. And that young people can make the right decisions based on that information."

Nevertheless, technology hasn't quite caught up with Shamp's project. He says less than 5 percent of the population owns cell phones capable of receiving the videos broadcast by his students. Currently, the videos are primarily available on YouTube. As technology evolves, however, Shamp believes it will become easier to get the videos to young people's cell phones.

Other projects using new media to provide information about sexual health issues include the 'KnowIt' campaign and HIV testing locator, a collaborative project between the CDC and the Kaiser Family Foundation. It allows users to text their zip code to "KnowIt" (566948) and receive a text message identifying the location of a nearby HIV testing center. Those without cell phones can receive the same information online at *www.HIVtest.org.*

In California, ISIS partnered with the California Family Health Council and the California Department of Public Health to create a text messaging program called HookUp. To use the service, users text 'hookup' to the phone number 365247 and are signed up for weekly health tips. Each tip provides information to help users locate local clinics for STD testing and reproductive health services.

Inspot.org, also run by ISIS, operates in 12 states and 12 metropolitan areas to allow users to find local STD testing resources. It also permits users who are diagnosed with an STD to notify past sex partners so they can be tested. The infected person has the option of remaining anonymous, as 80 percent of the site's users do, according to Levine of ISIS.

Kachur with the CDC believes policymakers are missing a tremendous opportunity if they don't use new media for STD and pregnancy prevention programs.

"I think in any health promotion program that has any money going into any policy related to STD prevention or pregnancy prevention, there should be a new media component to it," she said. "If you're going to do a health campaign, there should be a piece that provides funding for new media. . . . It can't be a novel thing anymore. It is what it is. Kids are the first ones to adopt it. If we want to reach them we've got to be in these places."

Society Does Not Support Teen Pregnancy

Heather Corinna

Heather Corinna is the author of S.E.X: The All-You-Need-To-Know Progressive Sexuality Guide to Get Through High School and College.

W hat I hate about that phrase ["preventing teen pregnancy"] is the patronizing, disrespectful and ignorant presumption that all teen pregnancy is unwanted or unplanned: it isn't, and while young women may have less information about and access to contraception than older adults [and] so may have more unplanned pregnancies than older adults (teens do have more unplanned pregnancies than older women, but the highest unplanned pregnancy rate right now is for those 18–24, poverty is as much a determinant as age is, and close to 50% of pregnancies for all women are unplanned), that part certainly isn't their fault or doing. Ask a young person what they want in sex education or contraception access, and you'll find it does not resemble what we, the adults who have withheld power from them in these policies, have usually provided.

Teen Pregnancy and Social Messages

I hate the shaming or demonization of teen parents or teens who become or are pregnant, the widespread assumption that all of that is always bad or always wrong, and must always be prevented based on anyone's standards but those of young people themselves. I hate teen pregnancy being presented as if it were a pandemic, and teen parents presented as automatically incapable of parenting just as well as anyone else. I hate the often-dishonest moralizing that often goes with all of this, and teens being told that all sex = pregnancy and that the only way to prevent pregnancy is to avoid all kinds of sex, and/or that choosing to be sexually active means choosing to be pregnant. I hate the other words so often used around this topic, which make teen pregnancy sound like Hurricane Katrina. I hate the defeatist messages we give teens or young women who have become pregnant and who are deciding to parent. I hate that we seem to hold teen or young mothers to higher standards of parenting than we hold older parents.

I hate that our culture has no problem recruiting young people into the military before the age of majority (for enlistment at 18, but the efforts start before then, contracts are often signed before then), suggesting that they have the capacity to make *that* kind of potentially life-altering decision, one that can often involve choices around life and death, and yet suggests they have no capacity to make this one. I hate that in many states and areas young women can be legally married at 16 or younger, and even though for the youngest teens, that often requires parental consent or a pregnancy, I hate that it's thought by so many that marriage at the age of 16 somehow makes young parenting easier, better or more socially acceptable, or that for a 16-year-old woman, a legally binding marriage contract is somehow less of a big deal, less of a limitation on her life, than a social contract to care for a child. I hate that there are states and areas which don't allow a young woman the right to choose to terminate a pregnancy of her own volition, and some which don't allow her access to contraception, and yet in some areas—especially when we are talking about nonconsensual sex—remaining pregnant is the only option we allow young women to have within their own control.

Ageism/Adultism

I hate the presumption that it is anyone's place *but* the teen in question to actually prevent a teen pregnancy. Can it be our place to help those who *want* help in that aim? Absolutely, and I hope that when and if any of us are asked for that help, we'll provide it. But it's not our place to *do* the preventing, because it ain't our body or our life. *It's theirs.*

Perhaps even more than that, I hate some of the attitude that seems to inform that presumption, which feels to me a whole lot like older people saying that it is okay for older women to become pregnant, but not for younger women. Which is a pretty odd thing to say about women who both have actively working reproductive systems, who both have the ability to become pregnant and to parent, or to make other reproductive choices. In fact, it sounds a whole lot like eugenics to me.

Few concessions are made to help a pregnant or parenting teen finish high school or enter college.

I'm not going to beat around the bush (as it were) here. In a whole lot of ways, women in their late teens and early twenties are in a better position than women in their thirties or forties are to reproduce, whether anyone likes it or not. They are more fertile, their bodies will bounce back more quickly from a pregnancy, and they have more energy both for pregnancy and for keeping up with small children. A 19-year-old woman and a 39-year-old woman, on average are not in the same space physiologically when it comes to bearing children. The younger woman, in general, is in the better, healthier position, and the same is likely so for her fetus, particularly if she has healthcare of the same quality the older woman has. And for most of human history—though there are certainly aspects of this, such as gender inequality and sexual violence, very worthy of critique and change—teen or young adult mothers have been who so many of our mothers were.

Resources Are Withheld from Teen Parents

There is another side of that coin, which is that young women are without some things many older women have. They more frequently will have less financial resources to care for children, their partnerships (if they are co-parenting) can tend to be less stable or shorter-lived, and they have less access to things like day care at school or work, good transportation, health insurance and the like. Obviously, too, a younger person has often had less life experience, and an older person may have greater perspective in certain areas which can be of great benefit when it comes to good parenting. But there are corrections for those inequalities. So many of the troubling statistics that we have on teen pregnancy and parenting aren't around the pregnancy or parenting itself, or the age of a parent, but instead, arise from many inequalities young people suffer because we have set things up so that they do.

Why is so much money put into developing and doing fertility therapies for women moving outside of their reproductive years, and so little for supporting women at the dawn of them?

For instance, it's not likely because someone is 16 when they become pregnant that they will be less able to finish high school, but because so many opportunities for schooling are cut off to young, pregnant women, and so few concessions are made to help a pregnant or parenting teen finish high school or enter college. Given the higher teen pregnancy statistics when it comes to young women of color, immigrant women and rural women, the fact that our culture often doesn't privilege education for those groups in the first place is no minor detail. It's not likely because someone is a teen that their child can be more likely to wind up in the corrections system, but because someone is a parent of any age who is without the resources they need to actively parent. Older people can help younger parents by sharing life experience and perspective gleaned with them rather than hoarding it or lording it over them.

Given that we know that that lack of resources is a central issue, why do we see so much money and so much effort put into "preventing teen pregnancy" yet so relatively little put into efforts to get free or affordable daycare into high schools and colleges, providing counseling, schooling and housing for young mothers? Why do we hear so much about preventing teen pregnancy yet meet so much resistance when it comes to contraceptive and abortion access for teen and young adult women? Why does the left and right alike tend to have so much to say and offer before or while a teen is pregnant, yet so little post-pregnancy or when a teen has become a parent?

Why is so much money put into developing and doing fertility therapies for women moving outside of their reproductive years, and so little for supporting women at the dawn of them; women of an age where even the best contraceptive methods, used perfectly, fail most often? Why are the celebrity teens or those of fame and wealth "speaking out against teen pregnancy" so often the loudest voices we hear? Why are the representatives of teen pregnancy and parenting so often so non-representative? Knowing about the disparities between white women and women of color with teen pregnancy, those between women in poverty and those who are affluent, and about the achievement limitations teens who choose to become parents so often feel they have, what the heck is up with the vast majority of those representing teen pregnancy being so wealthy, white and pampered (or male!?!) all the time?

Why are [adult male] efforts not put on talking to young men about sexual violence, sound sexual decision-making of their *own and contraceptive cooperation rather than in moralizing at young women?*

Pregnancy Politics

Knowing that for some teens who do choose to become pregnant, or risk pregnancy needlessly, it can come out of loneliness, the desire to cement a relationship, low self-esteem or the feeling that they have little opportunity for a breadth of life achievement, why do we shame them, blame them and put them down so often, further isolating those already isolated and low-feeling teens even more? (At the same time, it's important to recognize these are also often motivations or feelings of older women with pregnancy or parenting, too. They do not only belong to teens.)

For the many older men involved in these prevention initiatives, given the rate of sexual violence and coercion involved in so many teen pregnancies, given how often young men don't cooperate with sound contraception, and given the fact that no cisgendered man has any experience with being pregnant himself, why are their efforts not put on talking to young men about sexual violence, sound sexual decision-making of *their* own and contraceptive cooperation rather than in moralizing at young women? . . .

I'm also not entirely certain that there isn't, possibly, for some, some measure of envy at play here. It's tough to talk about, especially as a feminist, but I have had enough friends trying to reproduce at later ages now to know how incredibly frustrating the process can be for them. I also have friends honest enough with themselves and others that they will share that they do feel jealousy and anger when they see other women able to become pregnant as easily as breathing, and that's often the case with the youngest women. Some older women—not all or even most, but some—struggling to get pregnant now may even feel resentment about all the strong social messages they got about childbearing that they had to wait for later, should wait for later. If and when those feelings exist, they are valid and real, but don't have a place, covertly or overtly, in the discourse around teen pregnancy.

When older people and/or those of means are those creating the movements to "prevent teen pregnancy,"—and that is overwhelmingly who is—the onus is [on] us to evaluate and keep in check any bias we may have, and to be very sure those are not influencing how we treat teen pregnancy, planned or unplanned, wanted or unwanted. And that's what I think hasn't been done very well: that's what I see when I see phrases like "preventing teen pregnancy." I see a whole lot of bias, a whole lot of carelessness and a whole lot of disrespect.

Ageism is alive and well and teens are a very common— and often thought to be acceptable—target for it.

Time to Check-In

So, are we all checking in to be sure that older people aren't trying to claim some sort of ownership over pregnancy and parenting and who has the "right" to parent; who can and cannot be a good parent based on age alone—and nothing else—something we know has little basis in reality? Are we sure that some of the messages we're sending aren't about our own frustration or resentment; aren't coming from a place where we might feel like young mothers now are taking liberties we wish we would have? As well, are we sure that for those of us who felt that our lives went best because we did not procreate or do so at a given age aren't projecting our own goals and desires unto a generation which may be radically different than ours? Might we even be projecting some of what we saw and heard—and disliked—from our mothers generations unto this one?

Ageism is alive and well and teens are a very common— and often thought to be acceptable—target for it. We, as adults, make lousy policies for or around teens without allowing them input or control, and then we point the finger at teens when those policies we made or supported fail them, such as the poor sexuality education we've given them (especially in the last ten years here stateside), the awful relationship modeling, the glamorization, romanticism and commercialization of things like motherhood, vaginal intercourse, marriage and being sexually "attractive." The only real power we give them of late is in the commercial marketplace, and then adults whine about how youth are fixated on money and acquisition. Uh, okay.

Their sexual and reproductive lives are two of the areas where ageism is exercised constantly, and often without any resistance from even progressive adults. Are we sure that ageism and classism (not to mention racism and sexism) aren't playing a part in our discourse around teen and young adult pregnancy?

Are we also sure, that as can happen, that older people are not harboring a desire for their children to do *as* well as them, but not to surpass them? In other words, what if—just what if—a young teen mother really could "have it all"? What if she could be a good parent *and* finish high school, finish college, have the career she wanted, have all she envisions her life to be? By all means, that scenario might feel mighty frustrating for generations before who did not have the cultural or interpersonal supports or resources to achieve all of that, but not if we can see making things better for the generations that follow us as one of our great successes, not as something we were robbed of or must grudgingly provide.

Respecting Individual Choice

It stands to mention that some of this approach likely comes out of attitudes that are not just about young people or young women, but about pregnancy and pregnant women, period. We have long had a cultural problem with women's bodies and reproductive systems being treated like collective property; with laws, policies, practices and initiatives around pregnancy being led by everyone but those who actually are or will be pregnant. To some degree, the way we have been treating teen pregnancy is highly indicative of those attitudes, which isn't all that surprising.

But if we're serious about being pro-choice, if we're serious about wanting to help others make decisions in real alignment with respect and self-respect, the most basic foundation we have to hold is that every woman has the inarguable right to make choices about her own body for anything that happens to or inside of her own body, and that no one but that woman is most qualified to do so. Once we start talking about preventing a given choice someone else may make, we take that person's ownership of their choice away.

When our bodies are of an age where they can reproduce, any of us then—be we 16 or 36—has the right to choose to do that with our bodies if we want to. By all means, once a child is born, we're talking about someone else, someone outside of a woman's body, and not our own body. That's a huge and tangled discussion of its own, especially given the way children are so often framed as the property of their parents, rather than as the responsibility of parents and all the rest of us. But until there is an actual child born and independently present? We are talking about a woman and her own body. Not ours, *hers*.

For the record, I also have a problem with the notion of "preventing unplanned pregnancy." *A lot* of wanted children, children who are loved, children who are parented well, come from unplanned pregnancies: at least half of us have. As a sexuality educator who knows very well how many people don't understand how reproduction works, and as someone who has a good handle on human history per how long most people didn't know, it's safe to say *most* pregnancies throughout history have been unplanned to at least some degree. Even now when we do know more, when far more people are educated, when we have many contraceptive methods which are highly effective, a lot of people approach pregnancy not as something they exactly plan, but leave themselves more or less open to at given times depending on how okay they are with pregnancy. For sure, we do want to fill people in on the things which might make a pregnancy more or less healthy when it happens, make parenting go better or worse for everyone involved, but while planning can certainly contribute to healthy pregnancy and sound parenting, it really isn't a requirement or a reality for many people.

Words Matter

This really isn't all that complicated. Words matter. The phraseology we use for things matters, especially when we're talking about subjects like this. Especially when we are talking about choices which are not ours to make, about the lives of others and the bodies of others. Especially when we are talking about something as nuanced, complex and wildly individual as pregnancy and parenting. Especially when we are coming to something and saying that it is about quality of life and respect.

If your heart is in the right place, what you want to do is to not prevent anything. Rather, you want to nurture and support conscious conception and contraception, conscious birthing; to enable wanted and healthy pregnancy, wanted and healthy parenting. You want to help support all of us in having exactly the reproductive life we want and feel is best for us to the degree that we can control that.

If you're still stuck on prevention as an approach, why not try making it about *helping* teens to prevent *unwanted* pregnancy or unwanted parenting?

Is age really even relevant? Only so much. An unwanted pregnancy has the capacity to disrupt or cause hardship in a woman's life whether she is 17 or 37. A parent who is unprepared for parenting, who doesn't want to parent, or who just can't parent can do damage to a child no matter how old they are or are not.

What you really want to do—I hope—is to help women of all ages to understand what all their possible choices are for their whole lives, to have a good idea of what making any given choice can entail, the possible positives and negatives alike, and how it could impact them and others. What you probably really want to do is to help young people, all people, make choices around sex, pregnancy and parenting which are most likely to result in a happy, healthy life, and the life any given person most wants for themselves and those in their lives. What you also probably want to do is work just as much towards creating a culture of support for those who do become pregnant—by choice or by accident—and choose to parent as you work to support those making different choices. And if you really want to help to prevent unwanted teen pregnancy, you need to make sure your efforts are directed just as much towards young men as they are towards young women.

I know for a fact that many of the people who use the current language around teen pregnancy are people whose intentions are stellar, totally laudable, and all about the good things I'm talking about here. So, why diminish or mislead those great intentions with words and phrases that undermine them and disrespect the population we're claiming to care so much about? Why use the negative when you're trying to support the positive?

MTV Reaches Out to Teens to Prevent Teen Pregnancy

Women's Health Weekly

Women's Health Weekly is a weekly newsletter that covers all aspects of women's health, from diseases and conditions to drug development and marketing.

This summer [2009], MTV [Music Television] brings one of the most controversial and thought-provoking topics to its viewers with the new series *16 & Pregnant*. With statistics showing that three in ten girls in the U.S. will get pregnant before the age of 20, the show will take an intimate look inside the lives of pregnant teenagers as they face the challenges that come with being a young parent and dealing with relationships, finance, school and other new responsibilities. . . .

According to the National Campaign to Prevent Teen and Unplanned Pregnancy, more than 700,000 teenage girls in the U.S. become pregnant each year. The vast majority of these pregnancies are unintended. Despite the availability of sex education and access to contraception, the United States has the highest rate of teen pregnancy and teen birth in the entire developed world.

Reality Shows Educate

"MTV has a long history of reflecting the lives of our viewers with compelling reality stories," said Tony DiSanto, President of Programming MTV. "*16 & Pregnant* follows the journey of six young women going through an immensely life changing experience at such a young age. Each episode tells a new, unique story and shows the real life challenges they face from dealing with family and friends to school and finances as new mothers. This is the real secret life of an American teenager."

16 & Pregnant will follow the lives of teenage girls for 5–7 months as they navigate the unfamiliar territory and uncertainty of being pregnant. MTV was able to capture every moment and reaction in real time, including some of the births and how the young mothers and fathers deal with new parenthood. The series tackles a variety of issues including marriage, adoption, attending school, and dealing with gossip. Cameras will continue to follow the teens for a significant time after the births to show how the new parents cope with taking care of their infants in addition to balancing adult responsibilities with teenage life.

The show provides an honest portrayal of the challenges of too-early pregnancy and parenthood.

"Given that the teen birth rate is on the rise for the first time in a generation, MTV's *16 & Pregnant* is extremely timely," said Sarah Brown, CEO [chief executive officer] of The National Campaign to Prevent Teen and Unplanned Pregnancy. "We applaud MTV for using their unique and compelling style of storytelling to bring this important programming to their devoted audience. The show provides an honest portrayal of the challenges of too-early pregnancy and parenthood. The stories in *16 & Pregnant* are full of hope, heartbreak, and real life consequences and should be a must viewing for teens nationwide."

Reaching Out to Teens

The National Campaign to Prevent Teen and Unplanned Pregnancy is working with MTV to support *16 & Pregnant*. In partnership with MTV, The National Campaign is creating viewing guides for each episode so educators, key organizations and individuals can use the show, which will be available rights free for distribution, as a platform to have an honest discussion around sexual health and pregnancy with teens. In conjunction with The National Campaign, MTV will reach out to thousands of individuals and organizations across the country that work in education, health, and sex education to promote the show and its resources. Additionally, The National Campaign will launch an online resource to support the show at *www.stayteen.org*, to answer viewers' most commonly asked questions surrounding pregnancy and provide young people with the information they need to be fully informed on this topic. "With the high incidence of unintended pregnancy and sexually transmitted diseases, it's more important than ever to reach young people where they are and with messages that resonate," said Tina Hoff, Vice President and Director, Entertainment Media Partnerships. "Through our longstanding partnership with MTV, we reach tens of millions of viewers every day with programming and other content to help them make responsible and safer decisions about their sexual health."

MTV will reach out to thousands of individuals and organizations across the country that work in education, health, and sex education to promote the show and its resources.

During the month of May, National Teen Pregnancy Prevention Month, MTV and The Kaiser Family Foundation's It's Your (Sex) Life campaign (*www.ItsYourSexLife.com*) will also highlight resources and information on how to prevent unintended pregnancy and educate yourself on contraception. It's Your (Sex) Life, which promotes responsible decision making about sex, offers insight into what to do if you think you could be pregnant, are pregnant, had unprotected sex, and how to choose and use contraception properly.

What Challenges Do Teen Parents Encounter?

Chapter Preface

According to the Florida State University Center for Prevention and Early Intervention Policy, "The children of adolescents are more likely to be born prematurely and 50% more likely to be low birth weight babies (less than five and a half pounds) when compared to the children of mothers whose age was 20 or 21 when they had their first child." Inadequate prenatal care is linked to premature births and low birth weight babies among teenage pregnancies. Prenatal care helps the mother and her baby stay healthy. During a series of prenatal visits, health care providers monitor the growth of the baby and the health of the mother. Through prenatal care, pregnant women can learn about what to expect during and after pregnancy and receive guidance on a variety of issues, including nutrition, gestational diabetes, genetic screening, labor and delivery issues, breast-feeding, infant development, parenting, sensible exercise, intimate partner violence, infectious disease, tobacco and alcohol cessation, and substance abuse.

Teens encountering pregnancy may delay prenatal care because they feel scared and isolated. However, reaching out to friends, family, and the baby's father for support can pave the way to a healthy pregnancy. "Having at least one trusted, supportive adult—someone nearby in the community, if not a family member—is invaluable in helping them get the prenatal care and emotional support they need to stay healthy during this time," according to the Web-MD article "Teen Pregnancy: Medical Risk and Realities." Pregnant teens can find support in their communities through schools, churches, community centers, health departments, and other social service providers. By confiding in others, pregnant teens are more likely to obtain the prenatal care they need from doctors, midwives, and nutritionists.

If a teen is in denial about her pregnancy, prenatal care may be delayed. An unwanted or unplanned pregnancy can result in denial of pregnancy due to perceived pressure from parents or society. Teens in denial often hide their pregnancies from parents, friends, and classmates, and miss out on medical care as well as social and psychological support systems. Symptoms of pregnancy include a missed menstrual cycle, nausea, fatigue, moodiness, exhaustion, frequent urination, and breast tenderness. The symptoms of pregnancy and their intensity vary from individual to individual. Failure to notice the symptoms of pregnancy can result in postponed pregnancy testing. Postponing pregnancy testing is also a leading cause of delayed prenatal care among teens. If pregnancy is suspected, it is important to immediately schedule an appointment with a health care provider.

Although some studies conclude that it is ideal for teens to delay childbearing, teen mothers can increase their chances of having healthy pregnancies and healthy babies by getting early and proper prenatal care. Most often, the earlier prenatal care is received, the better the outcome for both mother and child. The viewpoints in the following chapter further explore the social, psychological, and educational challenges teen parents encounter in modern day society.

Teen Mothers Are at Greater Risk for Depression and Repeat Pregnancy

Diana Mahoney

Diana Mahoney is a reporter for Clinical Psychiatry News.

Depression in adolescent mothers is linked to an increased risk of rapid subsequent pregnancy, and these findings should come as no surprise.

In a secondary analysis of data drawn from two consecutive longitudinal risk reduction interventions, Dr. Beth Barnet and her colleagues in the department of family and community medicine at the University of Maryland, Baltimore, discovered that depressive symptoms were associated with a 44% increase in risk of subsequent pregnancy among 269 predominantly African American and low income teens.

The study included 297 pregnant adolescents aged 12–18 who received prenatal care at one of five community-based prenatal sites. At enrollment, the teens underwent a baseline structured interview and were randomly assigned to a subsequent pregnancy prevention intervention or to a usual-care control. Research staff administered structured follow-up questionnaires at 1 and 2 years post partum.

Of the 269 teens who completed at least one of the follow-up questionnaires, 46% had depressive symptoms at baseline, the authors reported in the March [2008] issue of the *Archives of Pediatric and Adolescent Medicine*. Of the 245 teens who completed 2 years of follow-up, 120 experienced a subsequent pregnancy within 2 years of childbirth. Of the 24

Diana Mahoney, "Depression and Repeat Pregnancies in Teen Mothers," *Clinical Psychiatry News*, vol. 36, April 2008, p. 44. Copyright © 2008 International Medical News Group. Reproduced by permission.

who were followed for only 1 year, 9 had a subsequent pregnancy during that time, they wrote (Arch. Pediatr. Adolesc. Med. 2008;162:246-52).

"The hazard ratio of subsequent pregnancy was significantly greater among the 112 teens with baseline depressive symptoms," the authors wrote, noting that the increased risk remained significant even after adjustment for possible confounders, including age, education, Medicaid status, exposure to violence, substance use, and relationship with the baby's father.

This study is the first to demonstrate with longitudinal data that depressive symptoms precede subsequent pregnancy in adolescent mothers and might be a determinant of this. However, in context of the following data on depression and adolescent mothers, the results could have been predicted:

Depression is a well-known nonsexual antecedent of teen pregnancy. In a recent national study using longitudinal data from more than 4,000 middle school and high school students, depressive symptoms in boys and girls were predictive of subsequent sexual risk behavior, including condom nonuse at last sex, birth control nonuse at last sex, and multiple sexual partners (Pediatrics July 2006;118:189-200).

The hazard ratio of subsequent pregnancy was significantly greater among the 112 teens with baseline depressive symptoms.

Depression is common among adolescents. According to the 2001 Youth Risk Behavior Survey of more than 13,000 students, 28% of U.S. high school students reported severe depressive feelings (MMWR 2002;51[SS04]:1-64). In a 2005 report of the results from the Office of Applied Studies' National Survey on Drug Use and Health, the lifetime prevalence of depression among adolescents was estimated to be 14% (http://www.oas.samh-sa.gov/p0000016.htm#2k4).

Rates of postpartum depression in adolescent mothers are significantly higher than those seen in adult mothers. According to the results of a recent integrative review of the literature on postpartum depression in adolescent mothers by pediatric nurse practitioner Vanessa Reid of New London, Conn., the prevalence of postpartum depression among women of all ages is estimated to be between 20% and 28% during the immediate postpartum period, compared with rates between 53% and 56% among adolescents (J. Pediatr. Health Care 2007;21:289-98).

Depression can interfere with a mother's ability to provide emotional and psychological support and attachment, as well as proper and adequate nutrition and physical care for her infant.

Rates of postpartum depression among African American adolescents are nearly twice as high as those observed in white adolescents, according to the result of a 1998 report on the National Maternal and Infant Health Survey (Am. J. Public Health 1998;88:266-70).

Without a doubt, the odds are clearly stacked against adolescent mothers and, by default, their offspring. Multiple studies examining the impact of maternal depressive symptoms on offspring have shown that depression can interfere with a mother's ability to provide emotional and psychological support and attachment, as well as proper and adequate nutrition and physical care for her infant, according to Ms. Reid.

"The results of studies that examined the relationship between maternal depressive symptoms and child outcomes revealed negative feeding interactions, negative or less positive interaction behaviors, child problem behaviors in preschool, and general pediatric complications, including lower weight, shorter length, and smaller head circumference," Ms. Reid said.

In addition, "repeat adolescent pregnancy and birth are associated with poorer pregnancy outcomes, less educational attainment, lower future income, and greater dependence on public assistance," wrote Dr. Barnet and her colleagues. "Children born into families with short interpregnancy intervals are exposed to increased parenting stress and negative parenting behaviors."

Remission of maternal depression has a significant positive effect on the health and well-being of both mothers and children.

Numerous interventions have attempted to reduce rapid subsequent pregnancy in adolescents, but "none that I am aware of have specifically targeted depression," Dr. Barnet said. Instead, many such efforts have focused on such factors as access to contraceptives, education, and social support. The outcomes have been disappointing, she said.

For example, the subsequent pregnancy risk reduction interventions from which Dr. Barnet and her colleagues drew data for their secondary analysis comprised weekly or monthly home visits beginning during the index pregnancy and continuing for two years. The interventions were facilitated by trained paraprofessionals who provided parenting instruction, case management, and motivational interviewing. Neither of the consecutive interventions achieved their primary intervention goal, nor were maternal depressive symptoms affected, she said.

In contrast, research has shown that treating depression in mothers can improve mother and child outcomes. Findings from the Sequenced Treatment Alternatives to Relieve Depression (STAR*D) trial showed that remission of maternal depression has a significant positive effect on the health and well-being of both mothers and children (JAMA 2006;295:1389-98).

Although it is not known whether treating depression in adolescent mothers will decrease the risk of rapid subsequent pregnancies, "our findings suggest that depression may be an important malleable risk factor," Dr. Barnet said. As such, she noted, depression in this group needs to be identified and treated, and doing so requires the implementation of a model of health care in which multidisciplinary primary care teams provide care coordination across clinic and community settings.

Schools might be an important frontline resource in this regard. For example, although it was not developed to prevent subsequent teen pregnancies or to address maternal depression, the Cradle to Classroom program, piloted successfully in the Chicago Public Schools, might affect both. The comprehensive program, designed to develop parenting skills in adolescent parents, help them finish high school, and promote healthy outcomes for the teens and their offspring, includes extensive in-school academic, social, and health supports for young mothers and an intensive home visiting program for the adolescent parents and their babies.

Of the 2,000 or so teens from 54 Chicago schools who had babies in 2002 and who participated in the program, only five had a repeat pregnancy while still in school. Also, all 495 seniors in the program graduated, and more than 75% went on to 2- or 4-year colleges (JAMA 2003;290:586).

Improving outcomes for teen mothers and their children requires this type of comprehensive strategy, according to Dr. Barnet. She and her colleagues stress the need for protocols that incorporate systematic practice changes and collaborative care teams.

Male Teenage Fathers Must Know Their Rights and Responsibilities

Jessica Stevenson/About.com

Jessica Stevenson is a teen advice guide for About.com.

There is a lot of advice out there for girls who find themselves facing an unwanted or unexpected pregnancy but there is very little information out there for guys. It takes two to make a baby but all too often when the pregnancy is announced the guy gets lost in the confusion. But teen fatherhood is not something to be taken lightly and along with responsibilities to the mother and the child you have rights that you need to know about.

What Are Your Rights as a Prospective Father?

First and foremost you have the right to know for sure that you are the father. This is not only a right you have but it is a right that the unborn child is entitled to as well. While everyone is mixed up in the emotionally charged circumstances surrounding an unwanted pregnancy it is often overlooked or downplayed that both father and child have a right to know the truth about paternity. Understandably a pregnant girl may be upset when the subject of DNA testing comes up but it is not something you should ever feel guilty about requesting. You are not calling her sexual conduct in to question by wanting to know for sure that you are the father. You are not suggesting that she is bad or a liar. You are simply exercising your right to know for sure that you are the father and this is important because fatherhood is a life long commitment.

If you are the father you have the right to know your child and to participate in your child's life. You have rights of custody and access. You also have responsibilities. You have the responsibility to financially and emotionally care for your child. You have a responsibility to be present in your child's life and ensure that your child's needs are met. You have the responsibility to ensure that your child is safe and well cared for and is free from harm. You have the responsibility to make decisions that are in the best interest of your child. More on rights and responsibilities later, first let's look at the most important thing every prospective father needs to know about . . . how to know if they are really the father.

If you are the father you have the right to know your child and participate in your child's life.

How Can You Know If You Are the Father?

There are two ways to determine if you are the father, blood type matching and DNA testing. Blood type matching is the cheapest and simplest test but it does not determine paternity it only tells you if it is possible that you are the father. If the blood types don't match up there is no possible way you are the father and no other tests are needed. If the blood types do match up it only means that you could be the father and a DNA test will be needed to know for sure.

In order to match blood types you need to know the answers to three questions; what is the father's blood type, what is the mother's blood type and what is the baby's blood type? A baby's blood type is determined by the blood types of its parents and it is an exact science as to what possible blood type a baby can have based on the types of the parents. It may sound confusing but it is really very simple. The blood type of the baby is determined by a combination of its parents' blood types. If the baby has a blood type that could not be the result of the combined blood types of *both* parents then the paternity is usually called in to question (since in natural conception maternity is never at issue).

So what is the difference between a positive and a negative blood type match? Rh factor aside (which determines if the blood type is positive or negative and is not effected by paternity) a baby will have the same blood type as either its mother or its father or it will have a combined blood type based on the types of both parents. A negative blood type matching happens if a baby does not have the father's or mother's blood type or if the blood type that a baby does have is not a possible combination of the father's and the mother's. A positive blood type matching happens when a baby has the same blood type as the mother, the same blood type as the father or a blood type that is a combination of the parents' blood types.

Remember in cases of natural conception if the blood types do not match it is because the wrong father has been identified. If the blood types do match up the next step that should be taken is a DNA test as blood type matches only suggest the possibility, not the certainty, that the right father has been identified. DNA testing is much more complicated and expensive but in the end it is worth the investment and many private labs have payment programs available to make access to this test easier. Don't feel bad about wanting a DNA test, as discussed earlier both father and a child have a right to know the truth. The most accurate DNA testing is done using samples from all three parties; mother, identified father and child, but testing can be done with only samples from the identified father and child. While it is possible to test DNA before a child is born this is much more costly and can pose a risk to the unborn child. For this reason most DNA testing is done after the child is born.

Marriage, Adoption, and Fatherhood

Should you get married? The question of marriage under these circumstances is a very personal one but it should not be entered into lightly. The pressure to marry when an unwanted pregnancy occurs can be overwhelming but there are important legal ramifications that potential fathers must be aware of. In North America our system of law is based on British Common Law and under this legal structure a child born in wedlock (that is to parents who are legally married at the time of birth) is automatically presumed to belong to the husband. A legal father has the same rights and responsibilities as a biological father. If you marry a girl who claims you fathered her child and later find out that you are not the father it can be difficult and costly, not to mention emotionally devastating, to have your parental rights and responsibilities changed. It may be worth your while to consult with a lawyer near where you live before marrying under these circumstances in order to fully and properly understand the law on this matter where you live.

What about adoption? Can I give up my baby for adoption even if the mother does not want to? No, you can't force the other parent to give the child up for adoption. You may be able to give up your own parental rights however, depending on the laws where you live. A lawyer in your area can better advise you on the subject of giving up parental rights and obligations and if this is something you want you must seek legal advice.

Fathers are no less important than mothers and their obligations to their child are no less than those of a mother.

OK, I'm the father and I'm going to be involved, now what? If you and the mother can agree on a custody arrangement and on child support it can be as simple as signing an agreement and filing it with the family court in your area. This may or may not require a lawyer. When there is nothing being disputed by either parent then the matter of filing is relatively simple and any associated legal fees are usually minimal. If the two of you can't agree then you will need a lawyer. As a father you have the right to know your child and to be a participant in his or her life. You also have the responsibility to support and care for your child and if you are the non-custodial parent you have the responsibility to pay child support. As touched on earlier you have the responsibility to ensure that your child is free from harm and is well cared for. If you believe that the mother is unable to care for your child or that your child is being harmed in her care then you have a responsibility to do something about it. On the other hand, if a mother believes that you may be bad for the child or put the child in harms way then she has a responsibility to do something about it. This usually involves going to court to stop or limit access. A lawyer will be needed and depending on where you live you may be able to get legal aid or assistance. Check with your local law society, Attorney General or other public law office.

Parenthood is not an easy thing and it should never be entered into lightly. No matter what the circumstances surrounding conception, when you become a parent you are a parent for the rest of your life. Fathers are no less important than mothers and their obligations to their child are no less than those of a mother. Just because biology has made it that mothers carry the child in their body this does not mean that the mother is the most important parent. Both parents have important roles to play in the life of their child. While having a child while you're still a kid yourself is less than ideal, this does not make you any less a parent. Once you know a child is yours it changes your life forever no matter how old, or young, you are.

Teen Pregnancy Presents Obstacles for Teen Parents to Stay in School and Graduate

Colleen McCauley-Brown

Colleen McCauley-Brown is a health care projects manager at Philadelphia Citizens for Children and Youth.

Want to know how Philadelphia's pregnant and parenting teens fare in the Philadelphia school system? Unfortunately, nobody is systematically counting or tracking what happens to these thousands of young people and whether they manage to finish school.

Philadelphia counts 3,500 babies born to teenagers every year. An estimated 10,000 to 12,000 teen mothers currently are found in the city. While the School District partners with Communities In Schools of Philadelphia, Inc. which operates an effective program for pregnant and parenting teens, called ELECT/Cradle to Classroom, it serves only about one-tenth of that number.

The challenges faced by these pregnant and parenting teens in finishing school are complex. (This story is based in part on anonymous interviews with teen parents.)

As a pregnant, 18-year-old mother of one explained: "I was 15 and in the ninth grade when I got pregnant for the first time. I left Bartram High because another student assaulted me on school grounds while I was pregnant, and I didn't feel safe anymore. I stayed out of school for a year and the whole time I was depressed. I messed up my education by dropping out of school."

Colleen McCauley-Brown, "Pregnant and Parenting Youth: Do We Know How They Fare in School?" *Philadelphia Public School: The NoteBook*, Fall 2005. Reproduced by permission.

Undercounting the Population

While District reports show that some of the teens who drop out are pregnant or parenting, that number is very small compared to the number of teen parents in the city. Providing adequate services for these teens is difficult when there are incomplete data on whether or not pregnant or parenting teens are in school. Schools don't know who these teens are and cannot reach out to them to provide the supports they need to complete school.

School completion matters because studies show that without a high school diploma, young parents have a difficult time finding employment that will sustain their families. Without a diploma, teen parents are far more likely than their graduating peers to go on welfare or to live in poverty.

Providing adequate services for these teens is difficult when there are incomplete data on whether or not pregnant or parenting teens are in school.

Based on national data, anywhere from 40 percent to 80 percent of pregnant and parenting teens fail to obtain a high school diploma. The percentage span is so broad because so little tracking is done nationally around the educational attainment of young parents.

But teen parents are not invisible in the city's health and welfare systems. More than 90 percent of pregnant teenagers in Philadelphia do obtain prenatal care, from a health care system focused on helping young women have healthy pregnancies and positive birth outcomes. The state provides cash assistance for the child, and the child care system often subsidizes a large portion of child care costs.

Yet none of these systems count the young parents who complete school, encourage them to stay in school, or help with school support. Many of the staff in the health, education, and welfare systems are familiar with the challenges that may lead a young parent to drop out of school. However, these systems generally don't talk to one another—partly due to confidentiality laws and policies that restrict the type of information that can be shared and partly due to policies and practices that hinder collaboration.

The child care system helps with child care but does not capitalize on opportunities to help teen parents with school support.

Philadelphia's ELECT Program

ELECT, a state-funded program for pregnant and parenting students aimed at preventing dropouts, has been administered for the last 12 years [beginning in the early 1990s] by Communities In Schools of Philadelphia, Inc., which partners with the School District. ELECT provides case management, parenting and child development education, and home visiting services to pregnant and parenting teens.

The program has served between 1,000 and 1,500 students each year and currently [as of 2005] operates at 25 high schools—including all of the School District's neighborhood high schools. The ELECT program leadership reported a 70–75 percent average daily attendance rate among participants and a 98 percent graduation rate in the 2004–05 school year.

An 18-year-old Philadelphia mother of two from West Philadelphia explained what brought her to the ELECT program: "I dropped out after the birth of my first child three years ago when I was 15, and I finally did come back for my child. What kind of life was I going to have without a diploma? Was I going to flip burgers all my life?"

But state funding has stayed flat for Philadelphia's ELECT program for the last four years, and so ELECT reaches only a small minority of those potentially in need.

Issues for Policymakers

Local advocacy organizations such as the Maternity Care Coalition and Philadelphia Citizens for Children and Youth are working to try to identify pregnant and parenting youth and make it easier for them to stay in school or get back into school if they've dropped out. They have identified a number of other issues that state and local policymakers and service providers can address:

- The child care system helps with child care but does not capitalize on opportunities to help teen parents with school support.

- The state provides cash assistance for children but does not keep track of teen parents' school situation and encourage them to go to school.

- Because schools don't offer alternative options to keep up or to make up credits quickly, new parents sometimes have to repeat a whole year because they take three months to be with their new baby.

- Schools require parents to re-enroll a high school student under 18 who dropped out, making it more difficult for students to re-enroll than to drop out in the first place.

Michelle Hinton of the Family Planning Council added, "Schools and community organizations need to do better in providing counseling and supports to prevent teen pregnancy and then make sure we can assist them in staying in or returning to school."

Advocates say better data would move things forward.

"What gets counted gets attention," said Bette Begleiter of the Maternity Care Coalition. "We need to know exactly who these young pregnant and parenting youth are—both the teenage mothers and the fathers—so that we can better understand their needs and what helps or hinders them in staying in school.

"By keeping them invisible, they, their children, and the rest of us lose out," she said.

Teen Pregnancy Adversely Affects Each Member of a Family Unit

Kim Allen

Kim Allen is the associate state specialist and director of the Center on Adolescent Sexuality, Pregnancy and Parenting at the University of Missouri.

Much attention has been paid to the issue of teen pregnancy over the past fifteen years, with very good reason. Although the trend of unmarried births to teens has continually declined over the past decade, the need to get the message out that waiting until adulthood is best for all family members is still critical. Currently, the trend of births to young, unmarried parents is on the increase and there are serious concerns for all family members of pregnant or parenting teens. The number of single parent families has increased dramatically over the past few decades. Currently, more than half of all children do not live with both parents.

Like the national trends, Missouri teen pregnancy rates are on a decline, but there are still slightly more than 8,600 births to teens annually. Additionally, the rate of teen pregnancies for the Hispanic population is on the rise. From 1995 until 2005, the number of pregnancies among Hispanic girls increased by 140 percent, and the number of live births to Hispanic girls increased by 178 percent. At the same time, Caucasian girls are experiencing a slow but steady decline in rate of live births. The rate among African-American girls has declined most rapidly—going from a high of 109.8 per 1,000 girls in 1995 to a low of 71.6 by 2005. Rates among Caucasian girls dropped from 46.1 to a low of 35.9 per 1,000 girls.

Kim Allen, "Teen Pregnancy Trends in Missouri," MissouriFamlies.org, May 5, 2009. Reproduced by permission.

The teen pregnancy trends are improving, but the need to address the issue of teen pregnancy holds steadfast. The United States still has the highest rates of teen pregnancy, birth and abortion in the fully industrialized world. The effects of these pregnancies have a negative impact on the family system. In order to combat these negative effects, pregnancy prevention programs must continue to educate youth on the effects of pregnancy for the child, the teen and the family system.

The Impact on the Child

Children born to teen mothers are often at a disadvantage physically and socially. Children born to young, unwed, low-income parents are at a much greater risk for inadequate pre-natal care, low birth weight, and infant death as well as poor developmental outcomes. These children often have more emotional and social problems in childhood and adulthood. Children born to teen parents are also more likely to be abused or neglected, score lower in standardized testing, and are more likely to go to prison than a child born to an older mother.

Poverty is another concern for children born to teen moms. In Missouri, 35 percent of all children live below the poverty level, and 66 percent of those children live in a single parent home. The discrepancy between two parent and single parent families is severe—the poverty rate for children living in married households is 8.4 percent whereas for children living in female headed households it is 38.4 percent.

The Impact on the Parents and Family

Research shows that there are many advantages for teens to wait to become parents during adulthood. Teen parents are more likely to be unmarried, live in poverty, be depressed, alcoholic and commit suicide. A teen mother is at high risk for repeat pregnancy and not finishing school; teen fathers are more likely to be involved in risky behavior and earn less money throughout adulthood than married men who become parents.

These young parents are much more susceptible to depression and other mental health problems, have fewer economic resources and less opportunity for meaningful employment. Additionally, young mothers have less financial, emotional or parental support from the baby's father. Although most unwed young couples are interested in marriage at the time of the baby's birth, 80 percent of all teen parents will not keep a romantic connection with their babies' parent. For most low income, unwed parents, the reality is that they will live in poverty and raise their children with little to no contact with the other parent.

The implications for the high risk factors in health, mental health and economic wellbeing for teen parents creates a system that is more likely to fail for everyone involved.

The implications for the high risk factors in health, mental health and economic wellbeing for teen parents creates a system that is more likely to fail for everyone involved, including children from outside the relationship and extended families. The extended family is still the primary support for teen parents. Young pregnant or parenting unwed adults continue to live with their parents for an average of five years and they most often provide emotional support, housing, transportation, financial and childcare assistance for their child and grandchild. Some studies suggest that with good support from families, these young parents have an increased likelihood for positive parenting and child outcomes. The reality is, however, that these families are often stressed and unable to support the teen and infant's needs.

Pregnancy Prevention
and Parenting Programs

The good news is that teen birth rates have steadily declined over the past decade. Although the outcomes for teen pregnancy are often negative, there are strategies and programs that are working that can continue to improve the rate of births to teens. Although many children born to teen parents will grow up in single-parent families, there are also programs being developed that help adolescent parents learn to co-parent and gain other skills that will help them be successful after the birth of their baby. New generations of teenagers develop every few years, and the need for education and promotion of later life child-bearing is as relevant as ever. In order to make progress on the issue of teen pregnancy, teens and their families need to understand the consequences of early sexual activity and avoid early pregnancy and child-bearing. These fragile families are at greater risk for mental and physical health issues as well as poverty, making the need for pregnancy prevention and parenting programs as important as ever.

Day-to-Day Life Is a Challenge for Teen Parents

Amy Umble

Amy Umble is the religion reporter for The Free Lance-Star *of Fredericksburg, Virginia.*

Joe Wood sits on a twin bed, folding freshly washed pink bibs, striped sleepers and patterned dresses.

His girlfriend, Heather Aylesworth, rests nearby, playing with 3-month-old Lilly.

Joe wants to help Heather as much as he can, because she stays up late studying, then gets up before dawn with Lilly.

Heather spends her afternoons and evenings figuring out how to calm a gassy baby, navigating insurance and tackling the ever-mounting piles of laundry.

By day, the 17-year-old attends Riverbend High School, where she tries to maintain her grades with just a few hours of sleep.

At 19, Joe is out of school and has looked unsuccessfully for a job. He now plans to move to North Carolina, where he will live with family and search for work so he can support Lilly and Heather.

Beating the Odds

Their lives epitomize everything that teen parent educator Joan Gillis tells the youths who enter her Program for Teen Parents.

"I always say, 'Babies are beautiful. They're wonderful. But you're too young to have them,'" Gillis said.

She emphasizes that the program does not promote teen pregnancy but aims to help teen parents and their babies.

Heather found the program, which is run through the Rappahannock Area Community Services Board, last year [2009] after she became pregnant.

Program for Teen Parents helped Heather connect with community resources. She and Joe took free Lamaze classes through the program.

Gillis works with teen moms in Spotsylvania County. Program for Teen Parents lost its state funding in 2007, but Spotsylvania supervisors agreed to fund Gillis' position part time in the county.

Gillis goes into the schools to help teen moms graduate. She has been a substance-abuse counselor and has seen firsthand that moms who don't finish high school are more likely to get pregnant again and to turn to drugs.

Heather is determined not to be one of those moms. "Statistics show a high rate of dropouts," she said. "I'd like to prove them wrong."

For now, she raises Lilly in the Spotsylvania home she shares with her mother and stepfather. Lilly sleeps in Heather's room, a space now bursting with a crib, a Diaper Genie, a playpen and other baby paraphernalia.

Lilly usually sleeps through the night, waking at 4 a.m. Heather gets up, feeds the baby, rocks Lilly back to sleep and then gets ready for school.

She takes Lilly to a babysitter in her neighborhood and then gets on the school bus.

If you can barely take care of yourself, can you really take care of someone else?

It is not easy, but Heather knows the best bet for her future—and Lilly's—is to finish her junior and senior years.

She wants other girls to know how hard it will be. Heather said some teens plan to get pregnant, for various reasons.

"It's kind of scary," Heather said. "If you can barely take care of yourself, can you really take care of someone else?"

But Heather and Joe both say they wouldn't trade Lilly for anything—even if they sometimes wish she'd come a few years later.

Community Support

Heather said that they have more support than most teen parents get. They help each other through the difficulties of raising a baby during the teen years.

Joe and Heather also get help from church and other community efforts. Monday nights, the trio attend YoungLives, which helps teen parents. Heather meets other young moms at the programs she attends. They know all too well what it's like to hear people whispering about you, or to take a test after being up all night with a fussy baby.

The moms tend to bond, and they share outgrown baby clothes, advice and support.

Program for Teen Parents also helps Heather pay for child-care. The program pays half those costs for participants who keep their grades up and who volunteer to help with the program.

"They've really taken a lot of weight off our shoulders," Heather said.

An annual craft fair pays for the child-care assistance fund. Heather and Joe have been helping with the event, which will be held tomorrow at Riverbend High.

Last year, the program helped 23 parents when it received money from Spotsylvania County. Now, the child-care money comes solely from fundraisers, and it supports only three.

Gillis said the program would like to help more, but it's good for parents to work for the help.

She hopes the craft show, sponsored by YoungLives, will bring in enough money. The child-care program began in

2001 and has helped 111 teens in nine years. In that time, 104 graduated or received GEDs [general educational development degrees].

Gillis emphasizes that this is the aim of the program. It is not to promote teen pregnancy but to offer the best outcome for the youths once they become parents.

Gillis has noticed more teen parents in the schools than before. A recent report showed an increase in teen pregnancy nationwide for the first time in more than a decade. That study showed the increase in 2006, and preliminary data show the numbers continued to climb in 2007, according to the Centers for Disease Control.

Gillis wants to see those numbers go down. She also wants to help young parents such as Joe and Heather become successful families.

Right now, the young parents are trying to plan their futures. Joe will search for a job and hopes to join the military after Heather graduates from high school. They hope to marry then, too. After the military, Joe wants to go to college to learn graphic design. Heather would like to be a nurse someday.

"You don't lose your dreams when you have a child," she said. "And we've got a lifetime to do it."

Teen Pregnancy Often Leads to Dependency on Social Services

Sarah Brown

Sarah Brown is the chief executive officer of the National Campaign to Prevent Teen and Unplanned Pregnancy.

E ven though the teen pregnancy and birth rates in the United States have declined by one-third over the past decade, one in three girls still becomes pregnant by age 20, according to data from the National Center for Health Statistics and other official data.

What's more, the progress made by teens has not been matched by young adults. Half of all pregnancies are unplanned and more than one-third of these unplanned pregnancies are to unmarried women in their 20s. Not only is unplanned pregnancy common, but it appears that the rate of unplanned pregnancy has stalled—and increased for some groups—between 1994 and 2001, the most recent data available.

Reducing the rate of teen and unplanned pregnancy remains a tough sell to policy-makers, practitioners and the public. "The critical link between teen and unplanned pregnancy and a host of other critical social issues, including poverty, single parent families, child welfare and education is often overlooked," says Andrea Kane, senior director of policy and partnerships at the National Campaign to Prevent Teen and Unplanned Pregnancy. "But if we can work together to do more to prevent unplanned pregnancy in the first place, the jobs of many APHSA [American Public Human Services Association] members will be easier."

Sarah Brown, "Preventing Unplanned Pregnancy Makes Human Service Work Easier," *Policy & Practice*, vol. 66, March 2008, pp. 38–39. Copyright © 2008 APHSA. All rights reserved. Reproduced by permission.

After 10 years of attention to teen pregnancy, the National Campaign to Prevent Teen Pregnancy has expanded its mission—and name; now the National Campaign to Prevent Teen and Unplanned Pregnancy—to begin reducing unplanned pregnancy among single, young adults in their 20s.

It is estimated that every dollar spent on family planning services saves three dollars in pregnancy and birth-related costs for Medicaid alone.

Prevention Is the First Step

Here are four areas that offer opportunities to work on prevention and where some states and localities are taking innovative steps to do so.

Medicaid. Medicaid serves as a major source of funding for family planning. Since the early 1990s, 26 states have been granted waivers from the U.S. Department of Health and Human Services to expand the scope and level of coverage— from extending coverage of postpartum care to providing family planning services at no cost. The financial case for these waivers is direct—it is estimated that every dollar spent on family planning services saves three dollars in pregnancy and birth-related costs for Medicaid alone.

Maternity care is one of Washington state's Medicaid program's largest expenditures. The state estimates that 50 percent of pregnancies to women on Medicaid are unintended (unplanned). Unplanned pregnancies among women between 20 and 29 years old accounted for $97 million of the state's Medicaid expenditures for women who gave birth in 2006.

Temporary Assistance for Needy Families (TANF). Reducing the number of unplanned pregnancies may promote self-sufficiency and reduce the number of children growing up with single parents. This in turn is likely to reduce the number of individuals in need of TANF. A provision in welfare reform makes clear that states can use TANF dollars for pregnancy prevention. Thirty-three states are doing so.

The Larimer County Department of Human Services in Colorado allocates TANF dollars to the local health department for family planning program outreach, reproductive health education and for birth control supplies. This has enabled clinics to purchase more effective and long-term forms of birth control. Through Virginia's Partners in Prevention Program, TANF funds support community grants focused on reducing unplanned pregnancy among those in their twenties. Welfare offices in Washington state have partnered with local family planning providers to station family planning nurses in all of the state's Community Services Offices.

Child Support and Responsible Fatherhood. Involving men in family planning remains a consistent challenge. The child support system and responsible fatherhood programs provide an opportunity to educate fathers on the consequences of having another child. To borrow an example from the teen world, the Office of Child Support in the Texas Attorney General's Office helps teen guys (and girls) understand the consequences of becoming young parents.

Child Welfare. Leaving foster care with children of your own can only complicate matters. Data from three Midwestern states show that by age 21, more than half of young women and nearly one-third of young men who have left foster care are parenting by 21 years of age [or by the time they are 21 years old]. Washington state found that pregnant teens are over-represented in its foster care caseload and that rates of accepted child protective services referrals and out-of-home placements are higher for teen mothers than for older women who have given birth. Educational programs, messages, and medical services geared toward youth as they transition from care could improve outcomes for the young people, their families and the child welfare system. Michigan and Indiana have recently started initiatives on reducing unintended or unplanned pregnancy.

Sharing a Common Goal

Success in reducing teen and unplanned pregnancy will only occur in partnership with organizations like the American Public Human Services Association and their constituencies. And success will manifest itself in improved child and family well-being, less poverty, more opportunities for young men and women to complete their education or achieve other life goals.

CHAPTER 4

Should Parental Consent Be a Requirement?

Chapter Preface

President Richard Nixon signed Title X of the Public Health Services Act into law in 1970. Through Title X, federally funded family planning services are offered to everyone. The passage of Title X fulfilled Nixon's promise that, "no American woman should be denied access to family planning assistance because of her economic condition." Once Title X was signed into law, health departments, Planned Parenthood affiliates, hospitals, and other agencies offered family planning and reproductive services nationwide, regardless of the patient's income. The U.S. Department of Health and Human Services (HHS) distributes Title X funding. Services offered by Title X supported agencies include the distribution of contraceptives, pregnancy testing, family planning counseling, adoption referrals, and abortion referrals. Although Title X funding cannot be used to perform abortions, supported agencies are permitted to provide non-biased, medically factual information about abortions and referrals upon request.

In order to receive federal funding, Title X supported agencies must abide by federal guidelines and rules that outline and limit the approved uses of the funds. In 1978, Congress amended Title X requiring supported agencies to provide treatment to adolescents. In 1981, Title X was amended again. The 1981 amendment required Title X supported agencies to encourage family involvement when adolescents received family planning services. However, the 1981 amendment does not block adolescents from receiving family planning services if they choose not to involve their parents or guardians. Those opposed to the 1981 amendment argue that parents have the right to know if their child is sexually active or considering becoming sexually active. The 1981 amendment is criticized because the confidentiality law not only enables adolescents to obtain birth control without their parents consent, but also enables sexual predators to obtain contraception for their victims. Those opposed to Title X also believe the act weakens family values, encourages sexual activity among adolescents, and promotes abortion. Religious organizations criticize Title X because of the government's involvement in the distribution of birth control.

Supporters of Title X argue that the act encourages involvement of a minor's family in decisions regarding reproductive health care. Supporters also note that some teens do not have a supportive parent or guardian and contend that not offering confidential access to contraception would lead to higher rates of unwanted and unplanned pregnancies. Through Title X, women of all ages have access to birth control, in effect, preventing unplanned and unwanted pregnancies. Title X is believed to benefit not only this generation but also the next because it eases the burden on taxpayers for unwanted and unplanned pregnancies, reduces rates of abortion, and strengthens the workforce.

Finally, Title X has been recognized for reducing inequalities in access to family planning services. According to the Guttmacher Institute, in its study "Title X and the Family Planning Effort," "One of the United States' key public health goals has long been to expand access to contraceptive services to all those who need and want them, with a special emphasis on reaching those traditionally hindered in their attempts to obtain care by income or other factors, such as age or geography." Through Title X, adolescents are offered voluntarily confidential services, options for contraception, and counseling. Critics and supporters of Title X make sound arguments for and against parental notification in cases involving teen pregnancy. The viewpoints in the following chapter further examine whether parental consent should be a requirement for decisions involving teen pregnancy.

Parental Consent Should Be a Requirement for Underage Abortion

Health & Medicine Week

Health & Medicine Week is a newsletter for NewsRX, the world's largest source for health information.

L aws that require minors to notify or get the consent of one or both parents before having an abortion reduce risky sexual behavior among teens, according to a Florida State University law professor in Tallahassee, Fla.

Jonathan Klick, the Jeffrey A. Stoops Professor of Law, and Thomas Stratmann, professor of economics at George Mason University, came to that conclusion after they looked at the rates of gonorrhea among teenage girls as a measure of risky sex in connection to the parental notification or consent laws that were in effect at the time.

The researchers found that teen gonorrhea rates dropped by an average of 20% for Hispanic girls and 12% for white girls in states where parental notification laws were in effect. The results were not statistically significant for black girls. The study will be published in an upcoming edition of The Journal of Law Economics and Organization.

Incentives for Teens

"Incentives matter," Klick said. "They matter even in activities as primal as sex, and they matter even among teenagers, who are conventionally thought to be short-sighted. If the expected costs of risky sex are raised, teens will substitute less risky activities such as protected sex or abstinence."

In this case, the incentive for teens is to avoid having to tell their parents about a pregnancy by substituting less risky

Health & Medicine Week, "Abortion Notification and Consent Laws Reduce Risky Teen Sex," October 16, 2006.

sex activities. In doing so, the researchers say, the rates of gonorrhea among girls under the age of 20 went down.

"This suggests that Hispanic and white teenage girls are forward looking in their sex decisions, and they systematically view informing their parents and obtaining parental consent as additional costs in obtaining an abortion, inducing them to engage in less risky sex when parental involvement laws are adopted," Klick said. "Unfortunately, the data do not allow us to differentiate between the possibility that teens engage in less sex or they simply have the same amount of sex but are more fastidious in their condom use."

The researchers ruled out the possibility that teens simply substitute risky sexual behaviors for which pregnancy is not a concern, such as oral or anal intercourse, because these activities still could transmit gonorrhea. The use of birth control pills also would not protect against the sexually transmitted disease.

The incentive for teens is to avoid having to tell their parents about a pregnancy by substituting less risky sex activities.

Consent Laws

The researchers used data from the Centers for Disease Control to determine the rates of gonorrhea for women by age and race for the years 1981 through 1998. Gonorrhea rates for teenage girls were compared to those of women 20 and older whose behavior would not be affected by the notification and consent laws. Using the rate of gonorrhea among older women as a control, the researchers were able to ensure that the decline in incidence among the teens was not simply reflective of an overall decline of the disease in the state.

Forty-four states, including Florida, have adopted laws requiring minors to obtain consent or notify one or both parents prior to an abortion, but the laws have been blocked by the courts or otherwise not yet enforced in nine of those states, according to the Center for Reproductive Rights.

Parental Consent Should Be a Requirement for Distribution of Birth Control in Schools

Randy Alcorn

Randy Alcorn is the founder and director of Eternal Perspective Ministries (EPM) in Sandy, Oregon. He also is the author of numerous books, including If God Is Good, Heaven, Pro-Life Answers to Pro-Choice Arguments, Women Under Stress, *and* The Purity Principle.

A recent *Primetime Live* program covered public schools whose health clinics are now surgically inserting Norplant beneath the skin of teenage girls. The practice is controversial not only because Norplant is a five year birth control device, but because it is being implanted without the permission of parents. (Yes, parents. Remember us?)

One of those interviewed was a junior high school principal, who defended the distribution of Norplant without parental permission. Her most memorable statement was, "morality is one thing, reality is another." An interesting idea here, that we must keep morality separate from reality. Reality, of course, is everything. Hence morality is restricted to the realm of nothingness. Maybe a better approach for a school principal might be to make morality a larger part of our reality, so that our reality can become a better and safer one. (No wonder California polls showed that the highest support for school vouchers came from minority families, who are tired of sending their children off to school to get shot at and pick up a supply of condoms and graduate not knowing how to read. They'd love the option of choosing better schools for their kids, just like President [Bill] Clinton and I do.)

Randy Alcorn, "In Condoms We Trust," Eternal Perspective Ministries, 2008. Reproduced by permission. www.epm.org.

The move to Norplant is just the next step in the philosophy of the last few years that has resulted in condom distribution in many public schools in America. Never mind that studies show condoms fail to prevent pregnancy at least 16% of the time. Never mind one study indicates that among young unmarried women they fail 36% of the time. Never mind that there's a word for people who count on condoms for birth control—"parents."

There's a word for people who count on condoms for birth control—"parents."

Of course, these failure rates take on incredible significance when you consider there are only a few days a month a woman can conceive anyway. How effective will the same condoms be in preventing diseases that can be passed every day of the month? When you consider that an HIV virus is 450 times smaller than a sperm, the slightest flaw, the most minuscule hole is going to result in the escape of the virus.

No wonder when a convention of 800 condom-affirming sexologists was asked if they personally would have sex with a person who is HIV infected, even with full protection of a condom, not a single one said "yes." They know something our children should know. So why aren't we telling them? Telling them that there's also a word for people who count on condoms for disease prevention. That word is "infected," which in many cases will end up meaning "dead."

Our Surgeon General, Jocelyn Elders, adorns her desk with a "Condom Tree." Dozens of different colors of condoms hang from it. Elders refused to recall a huge batch of condoms she distributed to Arkansas teenagers (where the pregnancy rate measurably increased under her reign), for fear that it would undermine people's faith in the condom. Several months ago, "In Condoms We Trust" Elders made this memorable statement: "Driver education tells kids what to do in the front of the car, and we should be telling them what to do in the back of the car." She referred, of course, not to abstaining from sex, but to using condoms when having sex. (To her, it is a given that children will have sex.) It wasn't too much later the president's "AIDS czar" blamed the spread of AIDS on our "Victorian morality." Huh? Am I missing something?

What doctors know and our children should too is that wearing a condom does nothing more than remove a few bullets out of the gun's chamber. But when you're playing Russian roulette, eventually the one or two bullets left in the chamber are sure to kill you. Especially when taking out a few bullets makes you feel safer, so you can feel good about playing the game more often. Of course, the real solution is not to better the odds in Russian roulette, it is to stop playing it entirely. That means sexual abstinence, as curiously offensive as that concept seems to be in some quarters. How can anyone still favor the "wink and give them condoms" approach when both research and common sense tell us it has never done anything but help create the exact problem we need to solve.

We must offer them help in developing their self-control, help them to "just say no" to sex as we help them to "just say no" to drugs.

Since the government, with Planned Parenthood as its trusted Lieutenant, began its large scale sex education programs twenty-five years ago, teen pregnancies and teen sexual diseases have escalated. Planned Parenthood's approach has been tried. It has failed miserably. If I may use the "A-word," isn't it time to get more serious about abstinence? By serious I do not mean including abstinence on the list of approaches, then saying to our children, "of course, most of you are having sex, or you're going to be having sex by the time the term's over, so let's get real and focus on condoms and Norplant."

When three eighth-grade girls who were sexually active with numbers of partners were interviewed on the *Prime Time Live* program, [television reporter] Diane Sawyer asked them if they would do anything different if they could start over. All three said they would wait until they were married to have sex. For various reasons they were all very sorry. Like any good liberal, Diane seemed very surprised by this revelation, and didn't follow up on it at all. The central point of the program was the importance of schools distributing condoms and the merit of Norplant's five-year birth control solution. The program did not pick up on the girls' deep regrets at their lost virginity. It was the perfect opportunity—totally missed because of the presuppositions of the interviewer and producers—to teach the concept of "secondary virginity." If sexual activity for teens is psychologically harmful and physically dangerous, which studies confirm that it is, we must offer them a chance to go back, to start over with new values and new commitments. We must offer them help in developing their self-control, help them to "just say no" to sex as we help them to "just say no" to drugs.

Yet the amazing fact is that we have congressmen (guess who contributes heavily to their reelection war chest) lobbying against the paltry few million dollars recently set aside to teach our children abstinence, while giving unqualified support to the hundreds of millions of dollars given to "safe sex" programs. They should be ashamed of themselves. In the old days they would have been called dirty old men for encouraging children to be sexually active. I'm not sure they deserve to be called anything better now.

Recently Hollywood has gotten behind these safe sex programs. Yes, the same Hollywood which shows teenagers hopping in the sack with each other on a routine basis, which makes millions on teenage sex and violence films. Hollywood has an investment in this issue. If America raised a generation of people committed to say "no" to promiscuity, morals-of-an-alley-cat Hollywood would lose a lot of its appeal, not to mention revenues. Given its track record, when Hollywood supports one side in this debate, it should be enough to convince us to throw our lot with the other side. (Why is it so politically fashionable to be concerned about polluting rivers but so unfashionable to be concerned about polluting minds?)

I have never met a person who looks back in regret at having abstained from sex before marriage. But I have talked with many people who are sorry they didn't wait.

Various abstinence centered programs have sprung up across the country, and a number of them look excellent. Best of all, they give students a real choice. If they want to, they can choose the Hollywood way, the Planned Parenthood way, the way of "safe sex" Russian Roulette. But if they do they should know the profound physical and psychological risks. They should also know there is a another way, a higher way, a better way. I have never met a person who looks back in regret at having abstained from sex before marriage. But I have talked with many people who are sorry they didn't wait, who are plagued by comparisons and doubts and fear of disease and wondering if their marriage will last when both partners proved by their premarital sex that marriage was not sacred to them.

The key, as someone has said, is not "safe sex" but "saved sex." That's why on her thirteenth birthday I gave my oldest daughter a heart necklace with a keyhole, symbolizing a commitment to saving herself for one man, giving him the key to her body on her wedding night and not before. When my younger daughter turns thirteen in another few months, I look forward to doing the same for her. Of course, our children must own the conviction themselves, but it is our duty and privilege to encourage them to follow the Lord in sexual purity, which is not only for his glory, but for their good.

"Just say No" is necessary but not sufficient. We must teach our children to "Just Say Yes" to obeying God, self-control, fidelity and mutual respect. Alley cats and rodents regularly engage in sex with any available partner. What raises us above animals is understanding, insight, and foresight. We understand how life works, the long-range consequences of our decisions. Sex is not just something we do, it is someone we are. It is tied to our innermost being. Condom distribution and Norplant are just attempts to get away with acting like animals. Instead, we should teach our children how to act like people. That is, after all, what they are, isn't it? And if we teach them it's okay to act like animals in this area, why should we be surprised when they steal and rape and kill without mercy, behaving "like animals" in other areas as well?

The promises of "safe sex" of course, are proven false with every contracted disease and pregnancy when school condoms were in use.

One last thought. How long will it be before our public schools will be inundated with a flood of lawsuits? Those districts where Norplant is implanted under the skin without parental consent, when a single aspirin cannot be given without parental consent, are not just doing a disservice to children and their parents, but are setting themselves up for great financial risk. Since they have no money of their own, but only our tax money, all of us will pay for this. (This is good to remember when we are told we don't have the right to influence what goes on in our schools.) Any trial lawyer will tell you schools could be attacked on the basis of promises of safety which the consumer, the child, believed and expected to be true. The promises of "safe sex" of course, are proven false with every contracted disease and pregnancy when school condoms were in use.

Think about it. Following the lead of Planned Parenthood, schools are now distributing false information and/or defective products. Since the statistics clearly show this already, the schools cannot even plead ignorance or sincerity. No warning of risks have been distributed with the product. No warnings of possible defects in design or production. The reasonably foreseen risks are not stated, which is a direct violation of consumer protection laws. Plus, schools may be held liable for inaccurate, incomplete, and incorrect training in use of the product. Such lawsuits may become paradise for trial lawyers, collecting their commissions from the tragedies of betrayed children whose mistake was believing what they were told at school.

If we don't wake up to our personal and moral responsibility to our children, perhaps what will finally get our attention is the financial implications.

Not Requiring Parental Consent for Abortion Endangers Teenage Girls

William F. Jasper

William F. Jasper is a senior editor for The New American.

In California, no girl is safe. Most parents in the Golden State don't realize it, but they have been stripped of their right and ability to protect even their very young daughters against sexual predators, rapists, and abortionists. That is the effect of the defeat of Proposition 73, the Parents' Right to Know and Child Protection Initiative in California's November 8 [2005] special election.

Of course, California, like every other state in our nation, has laws on the book against forcible rape and statutory rape (that is, consensual sex between an adult and a minor who is not a spouse). But a coalition of politicians, abortionists, and the state's pro-abortion Big Media has conspired to subvert the law and give rapists free rein.

Statutory Rape

A study of 46,000 pregnant school-age girls in California found that 71 percent of the fathers were adults, with an average age of 22.6 years. There are tens of thousands of cases of statutory rape each year in California, which has the highest teen pregnancy rate in the nation. But if some 25-year-old predator lures your underage daughter into a sexual relationship and gets her pregnant, he has a very good chance of escaping prosecution in California. All he has to do is get her down to a Planned Parenthood abortion mill, where the baby—excuse me, "product of conception"—can be scraped, burned, or sucked out, without you ever being notified or consulted. What's more, even though the predator has committed a criminal act in having sex with your daughter and the "health provider" is required by law to report such instances of statutory rape, the rapist knows that Planned Parenthood personnel can be trusted to cover for him.

A study of 46,000 pregnant school-age girls in California found that 71 percent of the fathers were adults, with an average age of 22.6 years.

Need proof of Planned Parenthood's complicity in this crime wave? Go to *www.YESon73.net* and click on their "Shocking Audio Tapes!" page. *YES on 73* is the group that spearheaded the recent initiative campaign. They have posted on their website undercover audio recordings of staffers at more than 90 abortion centers throughout California (the vast majority run by Planned Parenthood) assuring a squeaky-voiced 13-year-old girl telephone caller that no one will tell her parents or authorities about her impregnation by her 22-year-old boyfriend.

Here's a snippet from the call to Planned Parenthood of North Highlands:

Girl caller: "I'm just like, my friend told me that since like I'm going to be 14 in March that they would have to tell my parents I'm getting an abortion, but my boyfriend's 22. Is he old enough to take care of it and they wouldn't have to tell anybody?"

Planned Parenthood: "Actually, as long as you're 12 years and older all your records are confidential and nobody can get access to them. So they would not tell your parents." Planned Parenthood in Sunnyvale went even further: "We wouldn't contact your parents regardless of how old you are."

And they don't tell anybody, not even the law enforcement authorities they are mandated to tell. How do they get away with this? Easy: the state's political machinery—legislators, big city mayors, prosecutors, courts—is dominated by militant pro-aborts, who are richly funded by Planned Parenthood's recycled blood money (millions of taxpayer dollars from government-funded abortions).

Minors cannot legally buy alcoholic beverages, cigarettes, or chewing tobacco. So why is there such a huge disconnect when it comes to abortion for minor girls?

Parental Consent

Most states in our nation have laws on the books that either prohibit tattooing and body piercing of minors, or at least require proof of parental consent for these procedures. Likewise, schools and hospital emergency rooms must obtain parental consent before administering so much as an aspirin to a child. If a teacher wants to take the students on a field trip, again, parental permission is required. Minors cannot legally buy alcoholic beverages, cigarettes, or chewing tobacco. So why is there such a huge disconnect when it comes to abortion for minor girls? Can any sensible person really believe that having an abortion is less serious, less dangerous, less emotionally and physically traumatic than taking an aspirin or piercing an ear, and therefore, less deserving of parental involvement?

Prop 73 did not even propose to require parental consent for minors to get an abortion, it only required notification of at least one parent at least 48 hours before an abortion can be performed on a daughter age 17 or younger. Thirty-four other states have enacted similar or more stringent parental notification or parental consent laws, with the result that teen pregnancies and teen abortions have dropped dramatically in those states.

But doesn't the fact that California voters—which includes parents—rejected Prop 73 by 53 to 47 percent prove that Californians don't see any need for parental notification? No, it merely shows that most California parents are still uninformed.

Planned Parenthood threw nearly five million dollars into its deceptive NO on 73 campaign and swamped the airwaves with misleading ads. In addition, they had support of the state's Big Media, which provided the equivalent of millions of dollars in sympathetic coverage. By contrast, YES on 73 spent only a little over $700,000. They had mostly hostile media coverage, when they could get it. So, in California, until voters sweep the blood money cabal from power, abortionists and rapists are winners—parents and daughters are losers.

Parental Involvement Laws Erode Abortion Rights for Teens

Lynda Zielinski

Lynda Zielinski is a retired licensed social worker and writer.

"Your Jane Doe is here," the secretary tells me.

In juvenile court, a Jane Doe is not a dead person: She is a pregnant teenager, under 18, who wants an abortion but doesn't want to tell her parents about it. Ohio law allows her to have a court hearing before a judge, who can grant permission for the procedure—a "judicial bypass"—without the parental consent required in this and other states.

The young woman's identity has to be kept confidential; that's why we call her Jane Doe. I am a social worker in the court's diagnostic clinic. I interview juveniles before their court appearances—Jane Does, Delinquents and Unrulies, as they are called.

The interview takes place in my closet-sized basement office. The only real bright spot here is a photo of my twin granddaughters in oversized, flowery hats. When I first started working here, I was concerned that the image might upset the Jane Does, so I considered taking it down. But I learned that it didn't matter. These girls are desperate to get on with the abortion, get on with their lives. They are undeterred by pictures of young children.

Before she meets with me, the Jane Doe has already cleared several other hurdles. First, she visited our intake department, located in one of the city's toughest neighborhoods. There she was given the phone number of an attorney, who will also serve as her guardian ad litum [for the proceeding]—someone to look out for her best interests. She was also randomly assigned to one of our courtrooms. This assignment will pretty much seal her fate.

The intake department and the court itself are open only on weekdays, 8:30 a.m. to 4:00 p.m. School hours. Except in summertime, Jane Doe will have to cut class to get here. Truancy—one of the court's major concerns for all other juveniles—becomes a moot point for these young women.

Jane Doe had to arrange a meeting with her lawyer, who's located somewhere within our large county. A few of the kinder-hearted attorneys will arrange to meet Jane Does at a place more convenient than their offices, or at least accessible to bus lines. The lawyers realize that time is important for pregnant young women: Any delay could put them into the second trimester, making the bypass more difficult to obtain.

At the meeting with her lawyer, Jane Doe would have brought proof from a doctor confirming her pregnancy—another expense for her. (The result of a home test is not permissible.) She also had to show that she has received pregnancy counseling and knows her three options: having a baby and keeping it, having a baby and giving it up for adoption, or having an abortion.

When she finally gets to me, I start with the usual question, "How did you find out about the judicial bypass?"

"I did some research on the Internet and then I talked to a school counselor," she tells me.

Good. She has sought out an adult for guidance. I will be asked to give my opinion to the judge on whether Jane Doe is sufficiently mature to deserve a bypass, and well-enough informed to seek an abortion without parental consent. The informed part is relatively easy: In front of the judge, she must simply be able to go over her three options, explain why she has decided on abortion and describe the abortion procedure and its health risks.

But the "mature" part is insane. Mature compared to an adult woman? To an older teenager? More mature than a teenager who has decided to give birth? Maturity is ultimately in the eye of the judge; there are no specified psychological or legal criteria.

Another kind of judge never grants a bypass, under any circumstance. This is because of the judges' religious beliefs.

In our juvenile court I have observed a number of judges, who fall into several categories. Each is guided by personal beliefs—not about maturity, but about abortion.

One type of judge believes that the agencies we rely on for pregnancy counseling don't give proper emphasis to the "pro-life" viewpoint, and so provides a separate list to the Jane Does. Judges in that category require them to visit one of these places and bring back some literature as proof, then quiz the young women on their errant sexual behavior. Nonetheless, those judges usually grant the bypass.

Another kind of judge never grants a bypass, under any circumstance. This is because of the judges' religious beliefs—which are then justified by finding the Jane Doe to be "immature."

Other judges grant the bypass only after delivering a stern and lengthy lecture. They are well-intentioned, believing in promoting family unity. "Don't you trust your parents, who love you and provide for you?" they might ask the Jane Does. I have heard this lecture many times. It is given regardless of the girl's actual family circumstances—an alcoholic mother, say, or a father in prison for rape. I caution my Jane Doe not to show anger toward this type of judge, even if what he or she says isn't true of her family. "You have to show that you are mature," I remind her.

Finally, we have judges who grant bypasses without my testimony. Their reasoning is that any minor who can navigate through all the appointments ahead of the hearing *has* to be mature.

My latest Jane Doe enjoys her life. She looks forward to skating lessons, the prom, a trip with Mom to visit a college campus. She's worried about her reputation: She is a role model to her younger siblings and has never been in trouble. She doesn't want to upset her mother, who trusts her.

Most Jane Does say they are seeking the bypass because they don't want to disappoint their parents. Some, from dysfunctional homes, fear that their pregnancy may exacerbate problems between their parents. Some worry that it will add stress to a parent with emotional or substance-abuse issues. A few worry that they will be kicked out of their homes. Still others are certain that their parents would support their abortion decision, but prefer to handle it themselves.

This Jane Doe looks at me with pleading eyes. "I've been a basket case about this," she says. "I just can't have a baby now; I'm not ready. My boyfriend's been accepted to college on a football scholarship. He said he would support me, no matter what I decide. He's a good kid. I don't want to ruin his life too." She starts crying, searching for tissues in her tiny handbag. "I'm not a slut," she continues softly. "I haven't slept around. I know we should have waited to have sex."

"How do you think you'll feel after your abortion?" I ask her. "Relieved," she says. I always ask this of Jane Does, and this is their stock answer. It is the response given most often by women of all ages who have chosen to have an abortion. Relief. Earlier, we had talked about the risks. I asked her, "Which carries a greater risk, having an abortion or giving birth?" and she got it wrong. The impression many girls have is that abortion is risky but having a baby is, well, *normal*. In fact, while the fatality risk is 0.1 per 100,000 surgical abortions at eight weeks or less in the U.S., pregnancy carries a fatality risk of 11.8 per 100,000. And what about psychological harm? Teens suffer much more stress as a result of carrying an unwanted pregnancy than they do from having an abortion.

It's a good thing she doesn't seem crazy or un-grounded—then she might have to have a baby.

Yet mandatory parental-involvement laws—designed to make abortions that much harder for teens—are now in effect in 35 states. In comparison, 34 states and the District of Columbia allow most pregnant minors to obtain prenatal care and delivery services without parental notification or consent. Furthermore, all 50 states and D.C. give all or most minors the right to obtain treatment for sexually transmitted diseases without telling their folks.

On the day of the court hearing, I tell the judge that Jane Doe is 16, a good student, involved in various sports and responsible enough to drive. I testify that Jane Doe is appropriate in conduct and demeanor. She appears forthright and credible. Her thought processes are clear and goal-directed. These are some of the pat phrases I use in the courtroom to make her appear reasoned and stable. It's a good thing she doesn't seem crazy or un-grounded—then she might have to have a baby.

Jane Doe is asked to describe the abortion procedure and the risks. All goes well. As predicted, this judge grants the bypass.

Jane Doe is all smiles. She thanks me and her attorney. She goes on her way looking confident; she has jumped through the last hoop. But she doesn't know how lucky she is: She got a judge who is kind and follows the law. I'm thinking, this Jane Doe believes she is the exception here—a good girl. But I see a lot of exceptions just like her.

Meanwhile, courts whittle away at abortion rights under the guise of protecting young women from harm. If they would say, "We love the innocent fetus much more than the pregnant teen," then at least they would be honest. In Ohio this September [2006], another obstacle was added to the bypass steeplechase: a face-to-face talk with the doctor to learn about the procedure a day before the abortion. Another expense. Are the other professionals, who were quite capable before of explaining abortion, no longer qualified? To make matters worse, the law also now eliminates a young woman's ability to obtain a bypass solely because she faces abuse from a parent or guardian.

The determined, middle-class young woman will still manage to do what is required to get the bypass. She will then finish school, and at some time in her future may have a baby shower and go shopping for adorable wallpaper and an educational mobile.

Meanwhile, those who can't ace the bypass procedure, or lack financial resources, may find their options severely limited—and their burdens greatly increased. If they don't opt for an illegal—and often unsafe—abortion, they'll be expected to stay in school, work part-time, get to doctors' appointments and prepare to give birth and support a child.

If only they could have shown they were mature.

Parental Consent Laws Restrict Teenagers' Access to Birth Control

Center for Reproductive Rights

The Center for Reproductive Rights is a global legal advocacy organization dedicated to promoting reproduction freedom for women.

Currently, no state or federal laws require minors to get parental consent in order to get contraception. Increasingly, however, proposals are being introduced to restrict teens' access to reproductive health care by calling for parental consent or notification.

Examples of Minors Who Would Face Harm

Teens in a variety of circumstances would be affected if required to obtain parental consent for contraception:

- A young woman seeking contraception from a clinic—birth control pills, DepoProvera, diaphragm—would be forced to obtain parental permission

- A minor who buys condoms at a pharmacy could be turned away without parental consent

- A teen who seeks emergency contraception because of forced or unanticipated intercourse would need approval, even though emergency contraception must be used within 72 hours of unprotected intercourse.

Two types of mandatory parental contact for contraception are sometimes proposed:

Center for Reproductive Rights, "Parental Consent and Notice for Contraceptives Threatens Teen Health and Constitutional Rights," November 1, 2006. Reproduced by permission.

- Mandatory parental consent would force teenagers to get permission from one or two parents before getting contraception.

- Mandatory parental notification would require young people to tell one or two parents about their plans to get contraception. Mandatory notification poses the same danger of discouraging contraceptive use by teens as does the requirement of consent. If a minor is fearful about discussing contraception with a parent, there is no difference between 'telling' the parent and getting parental permission.

Federal Programs Require Confidentiality for Teens

Two federal programs—Title X and Medicaid—protect teens' privacy and prohibit parental consent requirements for teens seeking contraception. Title X provides funds to states for family planning services; Medicaid covers health care services for low-income women. Both programs mandate that, in exchange for receiving monies from the federal government, health care services treat all patients confidentially, including teens.

Confidentiality can be a determining factor for teens deciding whether or not to seek contraceptive protection.

Attempts by states to implement parental consent requirements for contraceptive services that are funded by these programs have been invalidated when challenged in court. Courts find that the requirements impermissibly conflict with federal program requirements. Federal program rules mandating confidentiality preempt state efforts to make new requirements. Nevertheless, states have continued to introduce legislation that would mandate parental involvement in teens' private contraceptive decisions.

Parental contact requirements discourage teens from seeking contraception, even though they may already be sexually active. Confidentiality can be a determining factor for teens deciding whether or not to seek contraceptive protection.

Almost half of women in the United States have intercourse by the time that they turn 18. While the teen pregnancy rate today has dropped slightly in the past twenty years, almost one million teens become pregnant each year. A sexually active teen using no contraception has a 90% chance of becoming pregnant within a one year period, according to the Alan Guttmacher Institute.

Lack of contraception increases the chances of unintended pregnancy. Nearly 80% of teen pregnancies are unplanned in the U.S. Teen pregnancy rates are much higher in the U.S. than in other industrial countries—double the rates in England; nine times as high as the Netherlands. Lack of contraception also increases the possibility of exposure to sexually transmitted diseases. About three million U.S. teens acquire a sexually transmitted infection every year.

Parental Contact Laws Threaten Teens' Health

Supporters of measures forcing teens to notify or get consent from their parents argue that they promote the best interests of young women and improve family communications.

Some teens face violence or other severe consequences from parents as a result of informing their parents that they are seeking contraceptive services.

These arguments are out of touch with reality. These proposed laws threaten adolescent health and well-being. Even teens who could comply with parental consent requirements will face delays in getting contraceptive services. Additional clinic visits, missed school or work time, and increased expense will result.

Many young women live in nontraditional situations—with one parent, a stepparent, other relatives, or on their own. Contact with biological parents, if required by law, may be impossible.

Some teens face violence or other severe consequences from parents as a result of informing their parents that they are seeking contraceptive services. Minors fearful of retribution may forgo using contraception altogether, even though they are already sexually active.

Teens who seek contraceptive services are generally sexually active already. They benefit from meeting with health care providers, who can provide screening, counseling about sexually transmitted diseases, and education about other reproductive health concerns.

Several courts have found that state parental consent requirements may not be imposed on federally funded family planning programs. Where states accept Title X and Medicaid funds, they cannot require minors to obtain parental consent prior to using those services.

Minors have a right to privacy that includes their ability to use contraception.

The U.S. Supreme Court said in 1977 that denial of contraception is not a permissible way to deter sexual activity.

Courts that have addressed attempts to impose parental consent or notification requirements have found that these types of laws conflict with a minor's constitutional right to privacy.

Although states may require parental consent for a minor's abortion when sufficient alternatives, such as judicial bypass, are in place, the same reasoning does not apply to contraception. According to the U.S. Supreme Court, "The states' interest in protection of the mental and physical health of the pregnant minor, and in protection of potential life are clearly more implicated by the abortion decision than by the decision to use a nonhazardous contraceptive."

Access to contraceptive services is considered a fundamental privacy right and has remained so for over three decades.

Parental Consent Laws Discourage Teens from Choosing Safe Sex

Rebecca Vesely

Rebecca Vesely is a Northwestern University graduate and has worked as a regional health reporter at the Oakland Tribune.

This year [2005], congressional and state lawmakers will likely consider whether to require family planning clinics that receive federal funds to notify parents when teens seek birth control. Now, a new study suggests that such laws would result in more teens having unprotected sex.

Only two states—Texas and Utah—require clinics that are funded by the state to notify parents before giving teens prescription contraception such as the Pill and Depo-Provera. Three other states—Virginia, Minnesota and Kentucky—considered similar legislation last year.

In Congress, bills have been introduced every year since the late 1990s to change confidentiality rules at family planning clinics to exclude teens. This year, there is more support in the Senate for such legislation, reproductive rights advocates say.

"I suspect parental consent is on the to-do list for the coming year," said Cynthia Dailard, senior public policy associate at the Alan Guttmacher Institute in New York, an advocacy and research group that supports reproductive choice.

This week [late January 2005], a study conducted by the institute and published by the *Journal of the American Medical Association* of more than 1,500 young women under 18 in 33 states suggested that teens would forgo birth control if they needed parental consent. Nearly 1-in-5 female teens surveyed

Rebecca Vesely, "Teens Opt for Unsafe Sex, Not Parents' Consent," Women's e-News, January 20, 2005. Reproduced by permission.

at federally funded family planning clinics would either use no birth control or unreliable methods such as withdrawal if parental notification were required. Allowed multiple responses, 7 percent said not having sex would be one of their responses to a law requiring that they tell a parent that they were seeking prescriptive contraception. Forty-six percent would seek condoms as an alternative birth control.

"We know that kids wouldn't stop having sex," said lead study author Rachel Jones, senior research associate at the institute. "Instead, we would have more kids having unprotected sex."

Seventy percent of teens whose parents did not know they were at the clinic said they would not seek prescription birth control if parental consent were required.

Many Parents Know Teens Visit Clinics

Surprisingly, 60 percent of the girls surveyed said their parents knew they were visiting a family planning clinic. The younger the girl, the more likely her parents knew she was at the clinic. Persuading teens to notify their parents about their sexual activity and reproductive health is preferable to mandating it, Jones said.

"Family planning clinics are doing a good job of encouraging teens to talk with their parents about sex and contraception," she said.

Still, 70 percent of teens whose parents did not know they were at the clinic said they would not seek prescription birth control if parental consent were required. Among the reasons teens cited for not telling their parents they visited the clinic was a desire to be self-sufficient and a fear of disappointing parents.

The Guttmacher study supports the results of smaller state and city studies on parental consent and contraception. The study authors, however, admit that the findings are based on hypotheses of what teen girls would do, not what they have done in response to parental notification laws.

Groups supporting parental notification such as Concerned Women for America and the Family Research Council said the study was biased because the Guttmacher Institute is affiliated with Planned Parenthood, which operates family planning clinics nationwide.

Debate in Congress

The parental notification debate in Congress centers on clinics that receive federal funding through Title X of the Public Health Services Act of 1970. Title X family planning clinics must offer confidential care regardless of age. Title X funds 4,500 of the 7,000 family planning clinics nationwide. The clinics served nearly 1 million teens under age 18 in 2001. Texas and Utah prohibit the use of state funds for clinics that don't require parental consent.

Representative Todd Akin, a Republican from Missouri, introduced a bill in 2002 that would require parental notification at least five business days prior to giving contraception services to teen girls at clinics funded under Title X. Amendments including parental consent requirements for teens to access family planning services have also been introduced.

Supporters of parental notification say that allowing minors to keep their reproductive decisions secret erodes parent-child relationships and helps mask abuse. McHenry County, Ill., about 50 miles northwest of Chicago, has mandated parental notification since a 1997 case shocked the community. A 12-year-old girl who was being raped by her 37-year-old teacher received Depo-Provera shots at the county clinic. The teacher was making the girl's appointments and driving her to the clinic.

Rules under Title X did not allow the clinic to inform the young woman's parents that she was getting the contraception shots. The teacher, William Saturday, pled guilty to criminal sexual assault charges and was sentenced to 10 years in prison. He served less than half that sentence and is now living in the county as a registered sex offender.

"The Title X grant aided in his crime," McHenry county supervisor John Heisler told a 2002 Congressional hearing on Title X. "It is shocking to think that a federal grant program can circumvent our state code."

McHenry County now refuses about $50,000 a year in Title X funding so it can require parental consent. But the law intending to protect minors could have had an unintended consequence. The county teen pregnancy rate has increased since the policy was enacted, while the teen pregnancy rate in surrounding counties declined, according to a 2004 study in the *American Journal of Public Health.*

Dr. Vinny Chulani, director of the division of adolescent medicine at Orlando Regional Medical Center in Florida said in his experience parental notification can prevent teens from seeking needed medical care. He recalled diagnosing two 16-year-old girls with advanced cases of the Human Papilloma Virus that can lead to cervical cancer. He said neither girl has had treatment to prevent cervical cancer because they need parental permission.

"The distant threat of cervical cancer is easier to bear than the immediate threat of revealing their sexual activity to their parents," Chulani said.

Organizations to Contact

The editors have compiled the following list of organizations concerned with the issues debated in this book. The descriptions are derived from materials provided by the organizations. All have publications or information available for interested readers. The list was compiled on the date of publication of the present volume; the information provided here may change. Be aware that many organizations take several weeks or longer to respond to inquiries, so allow as much time as possible.

Advocates for Youth
2000 M St. NW, Suite 750, Washington, DC   20036
(202) 419-3420 • fax: (202) 419-1448
Web site: www.advocatesforyouth.org

Established in 1980 as the Center for Population Options, Advocates for Youth champions efforts to help young people make informed and responsible decisions about their reproductive and sexual health. The organization believes it can best serve the field by boldly promoting a positive and realistic approach to adolescent sexual health. Advocates for Youth publications include "Comprehensive Sex Education: Research and Results," "Responsible Education About Life (REAL) Act," and "Science and Success: Clinical Services and Contraceptives Access."

American Association of Birth Centers (AABC)
3123 Gottschall Rd., Perkiomenville, PA   18074
(215) 234-8068 • fax: (215) 234-8829
Web site: www.birthcenters.org

The American Association of Birth Centers has been the nation's most comprehensive resource on birth centers. AABC is dedicated to the promotion of the rights of healthy women and their families, in all communities, to birth their children in an environment that is safe, sensitive, and economical, with minimal intervention. AABC publications include Expectant Parents Learning Center articles and the "Birth Center" brochure.

American College of Nurse-Midwives (ACNM)

8403 Colesville Rd., Suite 1550, Silver Spring, MD   20910
(240) 485-1800 • fax: (240) 485-1818
Web site: www.midwife.org

The American College of Nurse-Midwives is the professional association that represents certified nurse-midwives and certified midwives in the United States. The mission of ACNM is to promote the health and well-being of women and infants within their families and communities, through the development and support of the profession of midwifery—practiced by certified nurse-midwives and certified midwives. ACNM publications include *Quickening, Journal of Midwifery & Women's Health*, and *The Advocate*.

Campaign For Our Children, Inc. (CFOC)

One North Charles St., 11th Floor, Baltimore, MD   21201
(410) 576-9015 • fax: (410) 752-7075
Web site: www.cfoc.org

The mission of Campaign For Our Children, Inc., is to develop research-based prevention messages and educational campaigns that encourage healthy, responsible decisions among adolescents and that raise public awareness about adolescent preventive health issues. CFOC's materials have been incorporated into prevention programs, schools, and community organizations in all fifty states and in other countries, such as Zimbabwe, New Zealand, Canada, Yugoslavia, and Germany. CFOC publications include *Abstinence Makes the Heart Grow Fonder, If I Don't*, and *We Will Wait—A Male Involvement Lesson Plan*.

Feminists for Life of America

PO Box 320667, Alexandria, VA   22320

.

(703) 836-3354
e-mail: info@feministsforlife.org
Web site: www.feministsforlife.org

Feminists for Life of America is dedicated to systematically eliminating the root causes that drive women to abortion—primarily lack of practical resources and support—through holistic, women-centered solutions. The organization is a non-sectarian, nonpartisan, grassroots organization that seeks real solutions to the challenges women face. Feminists for Life publications include *Raising Kids on a Shoestring, The American Feminist*, and *Pro-Women Answers to Pro-Choice Questions*.

Healthy Teen Network

1501 Saint Paul St., Suite 124, Baltimore, MD   21202
(410) 685-0410 • fax: (410) 685-0481
Web site: www.healthyteennetwork.org

Healthy Teen Network is devoted to making a difference in the lives of teens and young families. It is the only national membership network that serves as a leader, a national voice, and a comprehensive educational resource to professionals working in the area of adolescent reproductive health—specifically teen pregnancy prevention, teen pregnancy, teen parenting, and related issues. Healthy Teen Network publications include *An American Frame: Teen Pregnancy and Parenting, The Core Components of Supportive Housing for Pregnant & Parenting Teens*, and *Promoting Healthy Teens*.

Lamaze International

2025 M St. NW, Suite 800, Washington, DC   20036-3309
(800) 368-4404 • fax: (202) 367-2128
Web site: www.lamaze.org

Lamaze International is a nonprofit organization that promotes a natural, healthy, and safe approach to pregnancy, childbirth, and early parenting. Knowing that pregnancy and childbirth can be demanding on a woman's body and mind, Lamaze serves as a resource for information about what to expect and what choices are available during the childbearing years. Lamaze International publications include *Lamaze Magazine, The Official Lamaze Guide: Giving Birth With Confidence*, and *The Journal of Perinatal Education*.

March of Dimes
1275 Mamaroneck Ave., White Plains, NY   10605
(914) 997-4488
Web site: www.marchofdimes.com

The March of Dimes mission is to improve the health of babies by preventing birth defects, premature birth, and infant mortality. March of Dimes researchers, volunteers, educators, outreach workers, and advocates work together to give all babies a fighting chance against the threats to their health: prematurity, birth defects, and low birth weight. March of Dimes publications include *Pregnancy Baby Book, How Your Baby Grows, Newborn Care*, and *My 9 Months*.

The National Campaign to Prevent Teen and Unplanned Pregnancy
1776 Massachusetts Ave. NW, Suite 200
Washington, DC   20036
(202) 478-8500 • fax: (202) 478-8588
Web site: www.thenationalcampaign.org

The National Campaign to Prevent Teen and Unplanned Pregnancy seeks to improve the lives and future prospects of children and families and, in particular, to help ensure that children are born into stable, two-parent families who are committed to and ready for the demanding task of raising the next generation. The organization's strategy is to prevent teen pregnancy and unplanned pregnancy among single, young adults. The National Campaign to Prevent Teen and Unplanned Pregnancy publications include *14 and Younger: The Sexual Behavior of Young Adolescents, A Good Time—After School Programs to Reduce Teen Pregnancy*, and *Another Chance: Preventing Additional Births to Teen Mothers*.

National Fatherhood Initiative

20410 Observation Dr., Suite 107, Germantown, MD   20876
(301) 948-0599 • fax: (301) 948-4325
Web site: www.fatherhood.org

The mission of the National Fatherhood Initiative is to improve the well-being of children by increasing the proportion of children growing up with involved, responsible, and committed fathers. The organization's strategy is to educate and inspire all Americans, support concerned organizations and fathers directly, and engage all sectors of society around this issue. National Fatherhood Initiative publications include *New Dad's Pocket Guide, The 7 Habits of a 24/7 Dad*, and *InsideOut Dad*.

Planned Parenthood Federation of America

434 West 33rd St., New York, NY   10001
(212) 541-7800 • fax: (212) 245-1845
Web site: www.plannedparenthood.org/index.htm

Planned Parenthood Federation of America is the nation's leading sexual and reproductive health care provider and advocate. It works with partner organizations worldwide to improve the sexual health and well-being of individuals and families everywhere. Planned Parenthood believes in the fundamental right of each individual, throughout the world, to manage his or her fertility, regardless of the individual's income, marital status, race, ethnicity, sexual orientation, age, national origin, or residence. Planned Parenthood publications include *The Facts of Life—A Guide for Teens and Their Families, How to Talk to Your Child About Sexuality—A Parent's Guide*, and *Birth Control for Teens*.

Women, Infants, and Children (WIC)

3101 Park Center Dr., Room 520, Alexandria, VA   22302
(703)305-2746 • fax: (703)305-2196
e-mail: wichq-web@fns.usda.gov
Web site: www.fns.usda.gov/wic/

Food, nutrition counseling, and access to health services are provided to low-income women, infants, and children under the Special Supplemental Nutrition Program for Women, Infants, and Children, popularly known as WIC. WIC provides federal grants to states for supplemental foods, health care referrals, and nutrition education for low-income pregnant, breastfeeding, and non-breastfeeding postpartum women and to infants and children who are found to be at nutritional risk. WIC publications include *Infant Nutrition and Feeding Guide, 7 Super Things Parents & Caregivers Can Do*, and *Breastfed Babies Welcome Here: A Mothers Guide.*

Bibliography

Books

Katrina L. Burchett	*Choices*. Ashland, OH: BookMasters, Inc., 2007.
Elaine Chase, Ian Warwick, Abigail Knight, and Peter Aggleton	*Supporting Young Parents*. Philadelphia: Jessica Kingsley Publishers, 2009.
Heather Corinna	*S.E.X.: The All-You-Need-To-Know Progressive Sexuality Guide to Get You Through High School and College.* New York: Marlowe & Company, 2007.
Becky Fraser and Linda Shands	*Standup Girl: Take Charge of Your Unexpected Pregnancy*. Cincinnati, OH: Servant Books, 2005.
Pat Gaudette	*Teen Mom: A Journal*. Lecanto, FL: Home & Leisure Publishing, Inc., 2008.
Helen Holgate, Roy Evans, and Francis K.O. Yuen	*Teenage Pregnancy and Parenthood: Global Perspectives, Issues, and Interventions*. New York: Routledge, 2006.
Margaret O. Hyde and Elizabeth H. Forsyth	*Safe Sex 101: An Overview for Teens*. Minneapolis, MN: Twenty-First Century Books, 2006.

Jeanne Warren Lindsay	*Teen Dads: Rights, Responsibilities & Joys.* Buena Park, CA: Morning Glory Press, 2008.
Jeanne Warren Lindsay	*The P.A.R.E.N.T Approach: How to Teach Young Moms and Dads the Art and Skills of Parenting.* Buena Park, CA: Morning Glory Press, 2008.
Jeanne Warren Lindsay and Jean Brunelli	*Nurturing Your Newborn: Young Parents' Guide to Baby's First Month.* Buena Park, CA: Morning Glory Press, 2005.
Maureen Lyon and Christina Breda Antoniades	*My Teen Has Had Sex, Now What Do I Do?: How to Help Teens Make Safe, Sensible, Self-Reliant Choices When They've Already Said "Yes."* Beverly, MA: Fair Winds Press, 2009.
Peyton Mathie	*Incubator Views: A Story of Teen Pregnancy and the Struggle of Her Preemie.* Lincoln, NE: iUniverse, Inc., 2005.
Joe S. McIlhaney	*Hooked: New Science on How Casual Sex Is Affecting Our Children.* Chicago: Northfield Publishing, 2008.
John C. Motley	*Talking to Teen Boys About Sex: What He Needs to Know Now!* Bloomington, IN: Author House, 2009.
Linda Ellen Perry	*How to Survive Your Teen's Pregnancy.* Dumfries, VA: Chalfont Publications, 2007.

Mark D. Regnerus *Forbidden Fruit: Sex & Religion in the Lives of American Teenagers.* New York: Oxford University Press, 2007.

Patricia Roles *Facing Teenage Pregnancy: A Handbook for the Pregnant Teen.* Washington, DC: CWLA Press, 2005.

Stephen Wallace *Reality Gap: Alcohol, Drugs, and Sex, What Parents Don't Know and Teens Aren't Telling.* New York: Union Square Press, 2008.

Ruth K. Westheimer *Dr. Ruth's Guide to Teens and Sex Today: From Social Networking to Friends with Benefits.* New York: Teachers College Press, 2008.

Periodicals

Shay Bilchik and Rene Wilson-Simmons "Preventing Teen Pregnancy Among Youth in Foster Care," *Policy & Practice of Public Human Services,* April 2010.

Heather D. Boonstra "Key Questions for Consideration as a New Federal Teen Pregnancy Prevention Initiative Is Implemented," *Guttmacher Policy Review,* Winter 2010.

Sarah Brown "Preventing Teen & Unplanned Pregnancy," *Policy & Practice of Public Human Services,* April 2010.

Robert Finn	"Slight Uptick Seen in Teen Pregnancy Rates: Increase Unlikely to Be Due Solely to Increase in Abstinence-Only Sex Education, Experts Say," *Ob.Gyn.News*, March 2010.
Ruth Garbutt	"Plain Speaking About Sex," *Community Living*, Winter 2009.
Lianne George	"You're Teaching Our Kids What? The Latest Buzzword in High School Sex Ed Class Is 'Pleasure'—Not Everyone Is Pleased," *Maclean's*, September 14, 2009.
Linda Arms Gilbert	"The Teen Pregnancy Dilemma: A Different Solution," *Delta Kappa Gamma Bulletin*, Spring 2007.
Cathy Gulli, Kate Lunau, Ken MacQueen, and Julia McKinnell	"Suddenly Teen Pregnancy Is Cool?" *Maclean's*, January 28, 2008.
Kim Krisberg	"Teen Pregnancy Prevention Focusing on Evidence," *Nation's Health*, April 2010.
Gerard Lemos	"Give Parents an Incentive," *Community Care*, February 19, 2009.
Molly Lopez, Jill Smolowe, and Michelle Tauber	"Teen Pregnancy Growing Up Too Fast," *People Weekly*, January 14, 2008.
Todd Melby	"The End of Abstinence Only?" *Contemporary Sexuality*, July 2009.

Jessica Press   "The Secret Life of Pregnant Teenagers: Before You Even Graduate from High School, You or a Girl You Know Will Probably Become Pregnant. Here's What You Need to Know to Avoid Becoming Just Another Statistic," *Seventeen*, June 2009.

Roni Caryn Rabin   "New Spending for a Wider Range of Sex Education," *New York Times*, May 11, 2010.

Robert Rector   "The President's New Sex Ed: So Long, Love, Abstinence, and Marriage," *National Review*, April 5, 2010.

Denise Rinaldo   "The Tough Life of a Teen Mom," *Scholastic Choices*, January 2010.

Erik W. Robelen   "Federal Abstinence-Only Sex Ed. Program Revived; Instructional Approach Winds Up in Health-Care Law," *Education Week*, April 7, 2010.

Kevin Roxas   "Keepin' It Real and Relevant: Providing a Culturally Responsive Education to Pregnant and Parenting Teens," *Multicultural Education*, Spring 2008.

William Smith   "The Great Sex Ed Divide?" *Conscience*, Autumn 2007.

Mike Tighe   "Study Links Teen Pregnancy to Sex on TV Shows," *Newsmax*, November 3, 2008.

Kelly White   "When You Least Expect It," *Girls' Life*, February–March, 2008.

Index